PENGUIN PLAYS

CHICKEN *and* AMBULANCE

Gregory Motton was born in Luton. He went to comprehensive schools and attended a university briefly. He has lived in Mexico City, Ballycommorraugh and London. He is twenty-five.

Gregory Motton

Chicken
and
Ambulance

PENGUIN BOOKS

Penguin Books Ltd, 27 Wrights Lane, London W8 5TZ (Publishing and Editorial)
and Harmondsworth, Middlesex, England (Distribution and Warehouse)
Viking Penguin Inc., 40 West 23rd Street, New York, New York 10010, USA
Penguin Books Australia Ltd, Ringwood, Victoria, Australia
Penguin Books Canada Ltd, 2801 John Street, Markham, Ontario, Canada L3R 1B4
Penguin Books (NZ) Ltd, 182–190 Wairau Road, Auckland 10, New Zealand

First published 1987

Made and printed in Great Britain by
Richard Clay Ltd, Bungay, Suffolk
Filmset in 10/12 pt Times

To Wander

Acknowledgement

Thanks to Michael Hastings

Contents

Chicken

Characters

The action takes place in an abandoned working men's cafe and in the street outside the doorway to where Sweet Lisa lives.

The jazz musicians are visible at all times and should be seated with their backs to the audience, behind the playing area. They are watching television while they play.

The first fringe performance of *Chicken* was at Portlands Playhouse in June 1986, with the following cast: Carol Bayford, Eva Carrol, Raymond Carty, Tim Holloway, Neil Packham, Bernard Pellegrinetti, Richard Self. Directed by Gareth Mills. Music by Roland Perrin.

Chicken was first produced at Riverside Studios on 9 April 1987 with the following cast:

BILLY	Paul Mooney
PAT	Christopher Guinee
DANDILION	Carrie Lee-Baker
MUSTAFA	Raad Rawi
MICHAEL	Paul Moriarty
SWEET LISA	Caroline Embling
MAN FROM THE COUNCIL	Richard Tate
JAZZ MUSICIANS	Richard Tate
	Dan Hildebrand
PLAIN-CLOTHES POLICEMAN	Dan Hildebrand

Directed by Kate Harwood
Designed by Brien Vahey
Music by Roland Perrin

A working men's café. Empty.

BILLY: All I want is two meals a day.

PAT: There's a lot of people want that.

BILLY: There's a lot of people get it.

PAT: I bet you haven't done an honest day's work in your life.

BILLY: I still have to eat.

PAT: Those who don't work don't eat.

BILLY: Yes they do.

PAT: Not if they've got any principles.

BILLY: I don't suppose you could tell me where I could get something?

PAT: I know a kitchen where they leave a slop bucket at the back door.

BILLY: Oh.

PAT: Do you want to join the party?

BILLY: No thanks.

[DANDILION comes in carrying a trumpet.]

DANDI: Excuse me is this yours?

BILLY: Yes it is.

DANDI: You left it behind, it was lying on the table, by your plate ... with all the other rubbish.

BILLY: Thanks.

DANDI: It's an expensive thing to leave lying around in cafés, are you sure it's yours?

BILLY: I think so, let me have a look.

DANDI: A look? What do you want to see it for, can't you tell?

BILLY: It's got my name inside.

DANDI: I think I'll put it back behind the counter. You can come back and claim it if you like.

BILLY: All right.

DANDI: Have you got any friends?

5

BILLY: Yes.

DANDI: Where are they?

BILLY: They're at home watching TV.

DANDI: How do you know?

BILLY: That's where they always are.

DANDI: How stupid. Why?

BILLY: Because they want to learn about things I suppose.

DANDI: And don't you?

BILLY: What?

DANDI: Want to learn.

BILLY: Of course I do.

DANDI: Then why are you hanging around here?

BILLY: I don't know.

DANDI: You should move on.

BILLY: Give me my trumpet then.

DANDI: All right. Are you sure it's yours?

BILLY: Yes!

[DANDILION hands it to him. BILLY plays his trumpet. The lights go up on the BAND who are sitting with their backs to the audience watching a very large TV set. DANDILION watches BILLY a few moments then walks off. Comes back in a couple of minutes when the music stops, wheeling a trolley. She stops in front of BILLY who stares at it in amazement.]

DANDI: I bet you'd like a chair too.

[BILLY picks up a morsel and eats. DANDILION fetches a chair. BILLY sits and begins to eat while she stands watching him. MUSTAFA and MICHAEL come in and seat themselves. MICHAEL is deeply dejected. MUSTAFA lights a cigarette.]

MUSTAFA: Don't cry.

MICHAEL: I'm sorry. [Handkerchief.]

MUSTAFA: I know it feels bad now but you'll wake up tomorrow morning, see the sun rise and suddenly life will be worth living again.

MICHAEL: But it won't be worth enjoying.

MUSTAFA: Think of all the suffering in the world. But you

6

and I have healthy bodies and strong minds. We've got food to eat, and cigarettes to smoke.

MICHAEL: Can you tell me what good is life without love?

MUSTAFA: Have a cigarette.

MICHAEL: Thank you.

MUSTAFA: Shall I order some eggs?

MICHAEL: I don't know, I'm not really hungry.

MUSTAFA: Oh come on. Four eggs! Four eggs!

MICHAEL: What time is it?

MUSTAFA: Between lunch and breakfast.

MICHAEL: Can you get me a cup of tea as well?

MUSTAFA: Four eggs, two teas!

MICHAEL: We were lying there in her room side by side. She was asleep. Suddenly there was a cry from far off, a human cry but you could hardly hear it. Somehow it woke her up. She turned and looked at me and for some reason I felt guilty. And then, all of a sudden we both realized she didn't love me any more.

MUSTAFA: What happened then?

MICHAEL: She threw me outside.

[DANDILION comes in.]

DANDI: All right, what do you want?

MUSTAFA: Four eggs, two teas.

DANDI: Four eggs, two – Do you want two eggs each?

MUSTAFA: Two each yes.

DANDI: That's not enough.

MUSTAFA: Why not?

DANDI: You'll get hungry.

MUSTAFA: All right. Four eggs . . . each.

DANDI: That's better. [Picks up empty cups and rushes away.] Won't be long.

MICHAEL: I walked the streets all night until I met you. I happened to pass her window while I was walking around and do you know what she did? She sent down this big brute to beat me up. Would you believe that? Only an hour or so before I had been lying in her arms.

MUSTAFA: So had he my friend.

MICHAEL: Please don't. Can't you look at this face I've got now. Look at my eye, it's all puffed up, I can hardly see.
[DANDILION comes in with food.]
DANDI: Four eggs. There you are love, and two teas. What's up with him?
MUSTAFA: He slept on his feet last night.
DANDI: That's what horses do isn't it?
MUSTAFA: And giraffes. Only they open their eyes every few minutes as well.
DANDI: What do they do that for?
MUSTAFA: To see if any lions are coming.
DANDI: You know a lot about animals.
MUSTAFA: Yes I was born on a farm. [Pause.]
DANDI: Oh well. Eat up quickly won't you, we're closing in a minute.
MUSTAFA: Closing? But it's lunchtime.
DANDI: And when do you think I'm going to eat my lunch? And besides there is something on television I want to watch.
MUSTAFA: Oh really, anything interesting?
DANDI: They're running the V E Day celebrations again, with subtitles for the hard of hearing. [Throws him a newspaper.] Here, read about it yourself.
[PAT comes in.]
PAT: Hello gents, mind if I join you?
[DANDILION brings him a chair.]
I saw you through the window. I was watching you.
MICHAEL: Yes I know, I saw you.
PAT: Did you?
MICHAEL: Out of the corner of my eye.
PAT: I got cold, I had to come inside.
MICHAEL: Never mind you can watch us more comfortably in here I expect.
PAT: Oh I don't care about comfort.
[DANDILION brings him a tray of food, not eggs but a lavish mixed grill, also a glass of water.]
[Tucking a serviette into his collar] Aren't you going to ask where I've been this morning?

8

MICHAEL: On the other side of this window, you told us
    already.
PAT: No, no before that.
MICHAEL: All right where?
PAT: I've been to the gym, I've been training my body.
MICHAEL: Well how's it going?
PAT: Marvellous. Look at these leg muscles.
MICHAEL: They're all right aren't they?
PAT: And that's not all I've been doing.
MICHAEL: What else did you do?
PAT: I've applied for a job.

Music uproarious.

£　　£　　£

**Lights up on the BAND who are still watching TV. A cold
windy day in early autumn, litter on the floor: a large pile of
black plastic bags filled with rubbish piled against a lamp-
post. BILLY walks along kicking a can until it lodges in a
newspaper. SWEET LISA rushes up to him.**
LISA: Who are you?
BILLY: No one.
LISA: Haven't you come to collect the rubbish?
BILLY: No.
LISA: Why?
BILLY: Why what?
LISA: Who's going to take it away then?
BILLY: I don't know.
LISA: I've been waiting for weeks, we've got rats.
BILLY: Oh.
LISA: It's because of the rubbish, it just piles up and up and
    no one comes to take it away.
BILLY: Oh.
LISA: You'd think they'd send someone ... I thought you
    were ...
BILLY: No.

9

LISA: Have I seen you before?

BILLY: No.

LISA: You're a bit young aren't you?

BILLY: What for?

LISA: To be collecting rubbish.

BILLY: I'm not.

LISA: I think you are.

BILLY: What?

LISA: Young.

BILLY: Oh.

LISA: What do you want then?

BILLY: Nothing.

LISA: Oh.

[She looks at him as if it was a strange remark. She stares at him a while in silence. BILLY grows self-conscious and tries to find something to say.]

BILLY: Do you live here then?

LISA: No.

BILLY: [Confused] Oh.

LISA: You can come up if you want.

BILLY: Up ... where?

LISA: Up there. It's not far. Do you like cats?

BILLY: Yes.

LISA: I've got seven. But three of them are dead, run over you see, it's too busy for them.

BILLY: Have you got anything to eat?

LISA: Don't know, I'd have to look.

BILLY: Would you mind giving me some food?

LISA: You'll have to wait there.

BILLY: All right.

[She goes to a doorway.]

LISA: Do you know any photographers?

BILLY: Why?

LISA: I want to be a model.

BILLY: I could ask around.

LISA: Don't bother. [Goes in.]

[BILLY sits on the ground leaning up against the

10

rubbish. Lights up on the BAND. They stop playing. One of them gets up and turns over to another channel. He returns to his seat and the BAND recommences. Lights back to the street where MUSTAFA and MICHAEL have arrived.]

MICHAEL: **[Pulling back MUSTAFA's arm]** Look where we've come to. No I don't want to, can we go back another way?

MUSTAFA: We're nearly there now. Hold your head up and ignore it. Have pride in yourself. You are a fine human being, you have nothing to be ashamed of.

MICHAEL: Oh Jesus look where he is, it's him who beat me.

MUSTAFA: He won't hurt you now. Please, this is the quickest route. We'll be there in a minute.

[BILLY gets to his feet and saunters over to them. MICHAEL stands apart, looking injured rather than cowed.]

BILLY: Excuse me have either of you got a bar of chocolate?

MUSTAFA: **[Tries his pockets.]** No, I don't think so. I'm sorry, do you need money for a bar?

BILLY: No it's all right I've got the money but I can't leave this spot, I'm waiting for someone.

MUSTAFA: I see, well perhaps we could buy it for you and bring it to you on the way back.

BILLY: Yes please. Will you be long?

MUSTAFA: We won't be long will we Michael? We're just going to find my friend here a new coat for the winter and then we're coming straight back. I think you may have met before?

BILLY: **[Looking at MICHAEL]** I have seen you somewhere before.

MUSTAFA: What do you want?

BILLY: Bounty.

MUSTAFA: OK.

MICHAEL: Could you tell me who it is you are waiting for?

BILLY: Em . . . I'm not sure what her name is.

MICHAEL: Oh you're not? Would you like me to tell you?

BILLY: Yes please.

MICHAEL: Sweet Lisa is her name if you can believe that. Well I wish you all the luck in the world with her. Here come on shake hands. I'm not afraid of you now!

BILLY: Yes, thank you, thank you very much.

MICHAEL: Come on now Mustafa let's be gone now out of here before she comes out and sees us.

BILLY: Don't forget my Bounty.

MICHAEL: Oh we won't my lad don't worry.

They go off. [BILLY returns to the piles of rubbish and sits. DANDILION comes in carrying the trumpet, runs into PAT who arrives at the same time. He stops her.]

PAT: Where are you going with that?

DANDI: I'm taking it to that boy.

PAT: Which boy?

DANDI: The one who left it behind.

PAT: What does he look like?

DANDI: He's about this tall and he was wearing no coat.

PAT: I know him. I'll give it to him.

DANDI: I wanted to give it to him myself.

PAT: What for?

DANDI: I don't know, I'll tell him not to leave it behind again.

PAT: I'll tell him.

DANDI: He keeps leaving it behind. It's very careless, these are very expensive.

PAT: I know I'll tell him.

DANDI: You won't sell it?

PAT: What would I sell it for?

DANDI: Money.

PAT: I don't need money, I'm above money. Listen child I want to give that trumpet to a lady friend. You wouldn't deny me that pleasure.

DANDI: And if I wanted to give it particularly to that young man?

PAT: I'd break your nose.

12

DANDI: Can't you just lend it to her so I can give it to him afterwards?

PAT: I'll see.

DANDI: Oh all right then. Don't go spitting your dirty saliva into it.

PAT: [Taking it] Not after you've had your filthy hands around it I wouldn't.

[DANDILION remains where she is and watches where PAT goes.]

Don't stand there girl, haven't you got anything else to do?

DANDI: No I haven't.

PAT: Well I don't want you standing there watching me. Go away.

DANDI: What shall I do?

PAT: Go home and write a letter.

DANDI: Who to?

PAT: A famous barrister, your favourite football manager, anyone.

DANDI: I can't think of anyone.

PAT: Listen I'm in a hurry. Can't you watch TV?

DANDI: No it's been stolen.

PAT: Stolen?

DANDI: This afternoon, when I went to watch it, some men were carrying it off down the road, there were about eight of them, there was nothing I could do.

[DANDILION walks off. PAT goes to SWEET LISA's doorway and starts going up the steps running into LISA who is coming down.]

PAT: Ah there you are, I was just on my way up.

LISA: Hello . . . Dad.

PAT: Hello my dear where were you off to?

LISA: Nowhere.

PAT: I brought you a present. [Hands her the trumpet.]

LISA: Oh, thank you.

PAT: I thought you might like to learn how to play it. But if you don't want to you can have it as an ornament . . . in your half of the room.

13

LISA: I think it would look better in your half.

PAT: We'll see. Go on, try to play it.

LISA: I don't want to. Not just now.

PAT: Go on please.

LISA: I will I promise. But later.

PAT: Look I'll show you. Put it to your lips like this and then blow. [Does.]

LISA: Yes I see. It's very nice.

PAT: I knew you'd like it. Come on let's go upstairs and see where we can put it. I think it will look best on top of the TV.

LISA: Yes I think so too. You put it there and I'll come home and look at it later. But I must go now or I'll be late.

PAT: Late? Whatever for?

LISA: My music lesson don't you remember?

PAT: I'll go and try this in a few different places then.

LISA: Yes.

PAT: See you later. [Goes upstairs.]
[SWEET LISA walks off but BILLY jumps up and walks next to her.]

BILLY: Is he a friend of yours?

LISA: Sort of.

BILLY: I see.

LISA: Actually he's my father.

BILLY: Oh.

LISA: At least he says he is. He just turned up one day claiming I was his daughter. I'd never seen him before. Of course he could be.

BILLY: I see.

LISA: He lives with me now. Well, he's got nowhere else. His bed is behind a curtain.

BILLY: I noticed he gave you a trumpet.

LISA: Oh he's always giving me things like that. He gave me a harp, now I have to take music lessons.

BILLY: Would you like to learn the trumpet?

LISA: Not really.

BILLY: Oh.

LISA: But of course if I had someone who was willing to teach me . . .

BILLY: [Shyly] I play a bit.

LISA: Doesn't it burst your cheeks?

BILLY: I don't think so.

LISA: All right then.

BILLY: I'm sorry to bother you but did you find any food?

LISA: Oh no I forgot. Can you wait?

BILLY: Yes.

LISA: You can see I'm quite busy.

BILLY: Of course.

LISA: But maybe if I see you here again . . .

BILLY: *Coq au vin.*

LISA: Pardon?

BILLY: You can get it in packets, you just add hot water.

LISA: Do you like that sort of thing?

BILLY: Yes.

LISA: I'll try and get some then. See you.

[She goes. BILLY follows after having retrieved his can from the newspaper. MUSTAFA and MICHAEL come in wheeling a TV set.]

MICHAEL: I'm sure it's stolen.

MUSTAFA: Stolen or not it will show us everything in action replay, I don't want to miss anything this time.

MICHAEL: What if the real owner sees us wheeling it along?

MUSTAFA: Put your coat over it.

MICHAEL: What if it doesn't work? They weren't too keen to show it to us.

MUSTAFA: They were too busy that's all.

MICHAEL: Too busy watching their own television. They've sold us their old one. I don't think it's going to work.

MUSTAFA: Ah the State Opening of Parliament!

MICHAEL: I wouldn't get too excited over it, from what I remember there's not much action.

MUSTAFA: But what there is they show over and over again isn't that right?

MICHAEL: Are you sure you're not getting it confused?

15

MUSTAFA: You see it's more than just the State Opening of
   Parliament, it's almost a national institution.
MICHAEL: I didn't like the look of that lot. Eight of them all
   sitting there and not a word out of them.
MUSTAFA: So. Where is your friend for his bar of chocolate?
MICHAEL: He's gone off. I probably scared him. He knew
   he'd got off lightly. Lucky for him I am a pacifist.
   [MUSTAFA eats the bar of chocolate.]

£   £   £

Winter. Snow on the ground, a cold wind blows. Inside
the café there are a few old Christmas decorations. PAT
is wearing a suit and looks dapper. His thin hair is greased
back and he wears glasses. He sits at a table writing on a
card.
PAT: Right, put this up in the window.
DANDI: What does it say?
PAT: 'The window you broke costs £200. Vandalism. What
   for? May God forgive you.'
DANDI: What do you want me to put that up for?
PAT: What's wrong with it?
DANDI: I'd be embarrassed.
PAT: Put it up.
DANDI: The Christmas spirit didn't last long did it?
PAT: Why do you walk in that funny way?
DANDI: What funny way?
PAT: Like this.
DANDI: I don't walk like that.
PAT: Yes you do. It's offensive to the customers.
DANDI: What customers?
PAT: All of them.
DANDI: I don't care.
PAT: It puts them off their food.
DANDI: You're mad.
PAT: Walk normally.
DANDI: I think the customers like the way I walk.

16

PAT: I've heard them complaining. This isn't supposed to be a
strip club.

DANDI: You know what you can do if you don't like it.

PAT: This is Party Headquarters.

DANDI: So?

PAT: You do want to be in the Party don't you? Since we're
doing so well. I'm going to be interviewed on TV next
week. It'll be good publicity for your lunches.

DANDI: I don't know. I only joined for a joke. Then you
started threatening me, saying you'd tell people I was
backward. I never liked that.

PAT: And they'll believe me too. You can't hide it once people
know.

DANDI: Don't do that.

PAT: Do as I say then.

DANDI: I don't know if I'm that backward anyway.

PAT: Yes you are. What's five times five?

DANDI: Don't start asking me those questions.

PAT: Come on, five times five.

DANDI: It's the pressure. I can't think when I know you're
expecting me to get it wrong.

PAT: What's the capital of Uganda?

DANDI: London?

PAT: Stupid.

DANDI: Oh I don't know. But I'm not simple.

PAT: What's that black mark under your eye?

DANDI: I don't know, what black mark?

PAT: Your mascara has run, you've been crying.

DANDI: No I haven't.

PAT: Yes you have.

DANDI: I've been peeling onions.

PAT: Since when have you been serving eggs with onions?

DANDI: I was thinking of doing an onion sauce.

PAT: Don't lie. What've you been crying for? In love?

DANDI: No.

PAT: Who with? Me?

DANDI: No, certainly not.

PAT: Who then?

DANDI: A man, a nice man.

PAT: He must be foreign. What's his name?

DANDI: He's not foreign, he's English.

PAT: What's his name then?

DANDI: Mustafa. He's got a nice moustache and he's friendly.

PAT: How friendly?

DANDI: How should I know?

PAT: Find out and tell me.

DANDI: What do you want to know all that for?

PAT: I'm gathering information.

DANDI: What on?

PAT: Foreigners.

DANDI: Why?

PAT: Why? Don't be stupid.

[Pause.]

DANDI: Someone came looking for you here the other day.

PAT: [Busy at his sign] Oh yes.

DANDI: Said you'd half killed her boyfriend.

PAT: Oh yes.

DANDI: Told me all about you. She wasn't half angry. She told me you made her kneel down and pray with you every afternoon asking God to punish your enemies.

PAT: And why shouldn't he? I punish his.

DANDI: She said you get quite emotional sometimes. She said it's touching to see you. She said you have an altar in there and everything.

PAT: Yes.

DANDI: With a picture of the sun god on it.

PAT: That's right.

DANDI: And a map of Highbury.

PAT: Do you mind? I'm putting the finishing touches to this sign.

DANDI: Sometimes you make her kneel on all fours she said.

PAT: Had a *long* talk did you?

DANDI: She said you were always jumping out of doorways on to passing strangers and breaking their noses.

PAT: A lot of young men walk past our building.

DANDI: Yes?

PAT: Well they're not all strangers are they! You're so naive. You saw the girl, you saw what type she was. She's always inviting strangers up into our room and they keep hanging around for weeks on end. One of them drew a moustache on the sun god.

DANDI: She didn't say anything about that.

PAT: No, she wouldn't. She doesn't always take life very seriously. That's why I like to see her on her knees as often as possible.

DANDI: She told me she wanted to be a dancer. I'd like to be a dancer too. I wouldn't take my clothes off though.

PAT: You don't think you can keep them on do you?

DANDI: I don't see why not.

PAT: It wouldn't be art, that's why not.

DANDI: She said that if you do magic as well they let you keep your clothes on.

PAT: You could never do magic, your fingers are too fat. And you could never dance, your hips are too thin. You'd better forget it. Go and make some eggs.

DANDI: All right. How many?

PAT: [Stares at her.] However many the chicken has laid.

DANDI: It's not a chicken. You told me it was a rooster.
    [Pause.]

PAT: I was joking.

DANDI: Oh. [Goes out disappointed.]
    [Enter the BAND carrying their instruments and a TV set. They settle down at tables.]

PAT: Hey hey hey, what's going on here!

TROMBONE: Excuse me?

PAT: What do you lot think you are doing?

TROMBONE: We thought we'd have lunch.

PAT: You can't have lunch here.

TROMBONE: Why not?

PAT: They don't do them.

BASS: But it says on the sign outside 'Lunches'.

PAT: Yes that means outside. The sign isn't inside is it?

BASS: No.

PAT: Well then.

TROMBONE: Maybe we can order in here?

PAT: I wouldn't bet on it.

TROMBONE: [To the rest] What do you fancy lads?

BAND: [Severally] Eggs I think. / An egg would be nice. / A couple of eggs for me please. / etc.

[DANDILION comes in.]

DANDI: Did I hear someone place an order?

BASS: Can we order lunch in here?

DANDI: Of course you can.

TROMBONE: Can we eat them in here as well?

DANDI: Of course you can.

PAT: Nope. Too many. Makes it too noisy. And besides we don't know what you've got in those cases.

SAX: That's all right it's only our instruments.

PAT: Oh so you're musicians.

BASS and SAX: That's right!

PAT: That does it then. You're not getting anything here.

TROMBONE: Why not?

PAT: This isn't a strip club you know.

BAND: [Severally] That doesn't matter. / That's OK, we don't mind. / etc.

PAT: Get out of here.

DANDI: Don't chase them away! What are you doing?

PAT: I suppose you imagine they'll ask you to dance on the tables, well I told you, you're too thin.

DANDI: Nonsense, they're just hungry!

PAT: I've heard that before.

DANDI: Anyway I recognize them from somewhere, I'm sure I can trust them.

PAT: How many per cent unemployed in Tyne and Wear?

DANDI: [Cowed] All right.

TROMBONE: And we've em . . . brought something belonging to you.

DANDI: Oh yes?

20

BASS: **[Wheels television forward.]** Yes, we thought you'd be quite glad to see . . . this.

DANDI: My television!

TROMBONE: Yes. Sorry for the inconvenience. Ours broke down.

DANDI: That's where I recognize you, you stole my TV!

BASS: We're very sorry aren't we lads?

BAND: **[Severally]** Yes, really sorry about that.

SAX: Anyway there wasn't much on, you haven't missed much.

TROMBONE: Yes, he's right. Over the past few months the programmes have been getting worse and worse. Now it's politics and jubilees virtually all the time. Actually that's why we brought it back.

DANDI: I see, well thanks.

TROMBONE: So we thought we'd cheer ourselves up with a bit of food. You see we used to watch television all the time, we really liked it.

DANDI: So did I.

BASS: We're really very sorry we took your television but we were desperate.

DANDI: What will you do without it then?

TROMBONE: We've decided to leave all that behind us and go and search for our friend, our trumpeter. He left the band a few months ago and we're wondering how he's getting on.

BASS: He used to watch TV with us.

DANDI: What did he look like?

TROMBONE: He was about this high and he wasn't wearing a coat.

DANDI: I've seen him.

TROMBONE: Have you?

DANDI: He used to come here. He kept leaving his instrument on the table.

SAX: That sounds like him.

BASS: Did he say where he was staying?

DANDI: No.

PAT: What makes you think he's the same trumpeter? The world's full of trumpeters. I've seen the one you're thinking of and he was twice as tall as this one they're looking for.

BASS: You can't tell. It might be him anyway.

PAT: What do you mean? Do you think he's walking around on stilts?

BASS: No but . . .

PAT: Well then, special shoes perhaps?

BASS: No, I just mean . . .

PAT: I know what you mean and I think it's highly unlikely. And if you don't believe us you can take your questions somewhere else.

TROMBONE: He didn't mean any harm.

PAT: What did you say?

TROMBONE: I said he didn't mean any harm.

PAT: So it's two on to one now is it? Look if you want a fight I'll take you all on.

SAX: Listen mate, don't get excited.

PAT: That's it, pick on an older man. Dandilion ring the police.

DANDI: Oh. [Goes out.]

TROMBONE: Look this is all just a little misunderstanding. It's our fault isn't it lads? We didn't mean to suggest that you weren't telling the truth.

PAT: I should hope not.

TROMBONE: No, we just came in for a few eggs and a cup of tea that's all.

PAT: I see . . . well you won't get any eggs here.

BASS: What? No eggs?

PAT: I ate the last one this morning.

BASS: Oh.

TROMBONE: That's a bit disappointing.

SAX: Are you sure?

PAT: There he goes again.

TROMBONE: Wait, wait, it's all right we'll just have a cup of tea each to take away.

22

PAT: Right! Fifteen teas to take away!

[From the kitchen the sound of a hen being chased.]

BASS: What's that?

PAT: What?

BASS: That noise. It sounded like a chicken.

PAT: Did it? I didn't hear anything.

[The noise again.]

TROMBONE: That does sound very much like a chicken to me.

SAX: You must have eggs!

PAT: I don't see why the presence of a chicken indicates eggs.

SAX: I bet you've got lots of bloody eggs!

TROMBONE: I think if you really have got eggs you ought to serve them to us.

SAX: We can wait for the chicken to lay the bloody things if you like.

PAT: Well you'll have to wait a long time!

SAX: Why?

PAT: I'll show you why.

[He goes out into the kitchen.]

BASS: What do you think he's going to do?

SAX: Where there's a chicken there are eggs and I'm getting hungry.

[Sound of squawking, a hen being chased then a gun shot and a final squawk. Pause. They stare at each other. DANDILION comes rushing out.]

DANDI: He shot it! He shot the chicken!

[PAT comes in from the kitchen.]

PAT: There! No chicken no eggs.

£   £   £

Winter. Outside SWEET LISA's flat. The black bags are piled higher and there is snow on top of them. A cold wind blows. SWEET LISA emerges from her doorway dressed very shabbily, her bright clothes are gone and she is wrapped in a worn-out raincoat: her legs are bare and she still wears summer shoes. Her face is pale and drawn and she hugs her arms around her. She stumbles across to the rubbish bags and adds to them a carrier bag of her own rubbish. Without looking round she makes back for her own doorway. BILLY appears.

BILLY: Hello.

LISA: What?

BILLY: Hello, do you remember me?

LISA: [Looks as carefully as the cold allows.] No sorry I don't.

BILLY: I used to give you trumpet lessons.

LISA: Oh yeah. Well what do you want?

BILLY: Nothing, I just thought I'd say hello.

LISA: Hello. [Turns to go in.]

BILLY: – and erm . . . ask how you were getting along.

LISA: Me? Oh fine.

BILLY: Good.

LISA: I must go in now. It was nice talking to you again, goodbye.

BILLY: I don't suppose you've got any food up there have you?

LISA: Food? No, sorry.

BILLY: I am extremely hungry.

LISA: Well don't ask me, I haven't got a thing. Go and ask someone else.

BILLY: I'd like to come in. Is it cold in your room?

LISA: Freezing. And you can't.

BILLY: Why, have you got someone else up there?

LISA: Yes.

BILLY: Who, your father?

LISA: No, I haven't seen him for days.

BILLY: Who then?

LISA: The man from the council. I phoned them about the rubbish and the rats and they sent someone round.

BILLY: Really? That's very good isn't it? What's he doing?

LISA: He's under the bed.

BILLY: Hiding?

LISA: No looking for rats. He's been there half an hour.

BILLY: Maybe he's fallen asleep.

LISA: Don't be stupid. The rats would eat him if he did.

[BILLY laughs.]

Something funny?

BILLY: No, I'm just cold, it makes me laugh.

LISA: Are you still wearing that bandage?

BILLY: Oh yes I am. Shall I take it off?

LISA: I don't care. How's your head?

BILLY: Much better thanks.

LISA: It should be, it was months ago.

BILLY: Your father packs a punch.

LISA: He's not my father.

BILLY: Whose father is he then?

LISA: How should I know?

BILLY: Why haven't you thrown him out then?

LISA: That's my business isn't it?

BILLY: Why doesn't he give you some money for a coat?

LISA: Bloody cheek! What do you think I am, some sort of tart? He doesn't keep me you know.

BILLY: He could buy you a coat anyway couldn't he?

LISA: Actually he doesn't believe in that sort of thing. He thinks you should help yourself.

BILLY: He can bend the rules can't he?

LISA: Of course not, he's a government minister.

BILLY: Is he?

LISA: He's been elected the secretary of state for sanitation and education.

BILLY: That's a good job.

LISA: It's very well paid. He bought a huge wardrobe the other day, it's so big you can hardly open the door to my room.

BILLY: What colour is it?

LISA: Brown. Very brown. There's a mirror inside the door but he's got the key.

BILLY: That's a shame.

LISA: It's a pity you can't come in. I remember now, we made friends didn't we?

BILLY: Yes.

LISA: Still that's how it often is, there's always a lot of things to keep people apart . . . I don't mind actually.

BILLY: No.

LISA: What have you been doing then all these months? I hope you haven't been hanging around here.

BILLY: No! I went to the coast. On a bus. I met some very nice people. We went and had some fish and chips on the pier.

LISA: That's nice.

BILLY: Yes, it's great by the sea. You can't swim in it though.

LISA: Why not?

BILLY: It's poisonous.

LISA: What a shame.

BILLY: And I joined a library, met some very nice old men in there, they lent me some newspapers. And then I met up with some other men. Oh yes. One of them knew you.

LISA: Oh.

BILLY: Yes he said you were . . . well he was a bit rude . . .

LISA: I know.

BILLY: But he was nice, very nice. And really interesting.

LISA: You've had a good time then.

BILLY: Oh yes. How about you?

LISA: Erm . . . all right. Actually very good. Really good. I met a photographer.

BILLY: Did he take any pictures?

LISA: No. He'd lent his camera to someone. But he said I was just right.

BILLY: What for?

LISA: I don't know. He was interesting.

BILLY: You've had a nice time as well then.

LISA: I certainly have.

BILLY: Do you still play the trumpet?

LISA: Oh no it killed my cheeks!

BILLY: You weren't blowing right.

LISA: Why didn't you teach me then?

BILLY: I have a communication problem.

LISA: Well it's too late now.

BILLY: Yes, I suppose it is. What are you going to do with your trumpet?

LISA: Do with it? What do you expect me to do with it?

BILLY: Mm. I don't know.

LISA: It's on top of the TV, why?

BILLY: Well I . . .

LISA: Do you want it?

BILLY: Yes please.

LISA: You can have it.

BILLY: Oh great, thanks.

LISA: I'll go and get it. [Goes in.]

[MUSTAFA and MICHAEL come in still wheeling a TV but now the screen has been knocked out of it and it is being used as a box. BILLY sees them out of the corner of his eye. Eventually MICHAEL notices him. MUSTAFA is in disguise.]

MICHAEL: Excuse me do I know you?

BILLY: Yes.

MICHAEL: I thought so. You're the one who sold us this television aren't you?

BILLY: Me? No. I've never sold anyone a television.

MICHAEL: Well, of course you couldn't actually call this a television. It never worked for us, not even once.

BILLY: I'm very sorry but it wasn't me.

MICHAEL: Caused us a lot of disappointment it did. Especially my friend here. In fact I don't think he's been the same since we bought it, it's like a burden to him, he's disillusioned.

BILLY: Sorry.

MICHAEL: Oh yes sorry. But you can't undo what's been done.

BILLY: I wish I could. Was it expensive?

MICHAEL: Expensive? Do you hear that Mustafa? Was the television expensive? Let me tell you how expensive it was. It cost this man a life-long dream to see the State Opening of Parliament, plus whatever you charged for it.

BILLY: I honestly didn't charge you anything for it because it wasn't –

MICHAEL: Come here, come here, take a look at this television, come on take a close look! Now tell me if you recognize it.

BILLY: Honestly I –

MICHAEL: Look at it.

BILLY: I ... oh.

MICHAEL: Well?

BILLY: Yes.

MICHAEL: Yes what?

BILLY: I do recognize it.

MICHAEL: Of course you do. Changed it a bit though haven't we?

BILLY: Yes you have.

MICHAEL: We've made it into a cocktail cabinet.

BILLY: That's very nice.

MICHAEL: Very nice. When you haven't got any cocktails.

BILLY: Maybe you can get some.

MICHAEL: Oh there's a chance. More chance than there is of seeing any programmes on it anyway.

BILLY: Yes.

MICHAEL: I suppose you've got your own television have you?

BILLY: No, no I haven't.

MICHAEL: Oh? And why's that?

BILLY: I don't know.

MICHAEL: Don't worry, I won't bear a grudge. Good people are scarce. Everyone you meet these days has got a funny handshake and keeps talking on about National Heritage. You can't trust any of them. My faith is in the young, even if they are dishonest. Why aren't you wearing a coat?

BILLY: Somebody stole it.

MICHAEL: That's typical, any idea who it was?

BILLY: The owner. He stole it back.

MICHAEL: Well he should be careful, you can end up in prison for anything these days. I knew a man kept pigeons all his life, ended up in prison.

BILLY: What does that prove?

MICHAEL: Nothing, but that's not what the judge said.

BILLY: Don't you remember we've met before? We travelled on a bus together.

MICHAEL: No, I don't remember that, but perhaps I'm getting you mixed up with someone else. With life being as it is I try to keep my memory as short as possible.

BILLY: You told me about a girl you were in love with.

MICHAEL: Love? Love is nothing but vanity, I have given up the search for love.

BILLY: You told me I should find a woman who would never leave me.

MICHAEL: Well, and did you find one?

BILLY: Hundreds.

MICHAEL: That was very fortunate, how did you manage that?

BILLY: I left them before they left me.

MICHAEL: Ah but you mustn't be cruel neither.

BILLY: It was you who taught me everything.

MICHAEL: Was it?

BILLY: Don't you remember? We went to a pub, the sweat was running down your nose. You were wearing your anorak.

MICHAEL: Nothing.

BILLY: Your eyes were shining with self-knowledge.

MICHAEL: Maybe I was drunk.

BILLY: You said you had a deep sorrow. Don't you still?

MICHAEL: I've no idea if I do or don't.

BILLY: You must be happy then.

MICHAEL: Not happy, merely suspicious. You can feed on suspicion but you can't feed on unhappiness. Take my friend here, one of the most trusting people in Western

Europe but he is unhappy. Consequently he hasn't a word
to say for himself.

BILLY: It seems rather complicated, I think I might go back
to Brighton.

MICHAEL: Have you got a young lady there?

BILLY: I left her on the front, we had been admiring the
chemical plant.

MICHAEL: Go back to her. This is no life for a young boy like
you. There's no freedom on the street corners any more.
Listen, I bet she keeps a nice little house there by the
roaring sea doesn't she?

BILLY: I never went inside.

MICHAEL: No, but you stood outside didn't you I bet?

BILLY: We sat on the wall.

MICHAEL: Well there you are then. And behind the wall there
was the smell of home cooking wasn't there?

BILLY: Em . . . yes there was.

MICHAEL: **[Seizing him]** Then what was it drew you away?

BILLY: She suggested we go for a walk.

MICHAEL: And then?

BILLY: We got to the sea and it reminded me of here, home,
freedom.

MICHAEL: Freedom?

BILLY: What I meant was, the tubes, the buses, you know.

MICHAEL: I see. Well you'll have to make the best of it now.
But whatever you do keep clear of trouble. God knows
there's few enough of us going to make it through this
winter.

[SWEET LISA comes down with the trumpet.]

LISA: Here you are.

BILLY: Thank you. **[Puts it to his lips and shyly plays a
few notes.]** Thanks, that's really great.

LISA: Well I never played it so you might as well. God I wish
that council man would go.

BILLY: I thought you were enjoying his company.

LISA: I was. But he talks about nothing but rats, he thinks
there are rats everywhere, he's going through all my

drawers now, he seems to think they might be hiding in there.

MICHAEL: I've never seen any rats at all in your room.

LISA: I beg your pardon? Who are you?

MICHAEL: It's so long since anyone asked me I've forgotten. But does it matter? Does it affect whether you have rats in your room or not?

LISA: Well I have!

MICHAEL: No you haven't. You were always complaining about rats, always jumping up in the middle of the night, 'Oh there's a rat under the bed get up; get up, there are his scuttling footsteps', but I looked and looked and there never were any.

LISA: Do I know you?

MICHAEL: We were never intimate.

LISA: You're making it all up. I don't know you from Adam.

MICHAEL: That's strange, my name is Adam.

LISA: No it's not it's Michael.

MICHAEL: Ah ha.

LISA: Oh.

MICHAEL: I know, we can all go up to your room and see if we can find any of these rats.

LISA: I'm not having that, there's no room. Hey, where's that man you used to hang around with?

MICHAEL: He's over there.

LISA: Why doesn't he say anything?

MICHAEL: Because he's too kind to accuse anyone. Things just go from bad to worse. You start off with all the enthusiasm in the world, you even buy yourself a broken television to watch it all happening in colour, and you end up wheeling an empty cocktail cabinet around and going in fear of your life, what do you expect him to say?

LISA: I don't see anything to be afraid of.

MICHAEL: What about that man in your room? What if he finds something in your cupboard, then you'll be in for it.

LISA: I've got nothing to hide.

31

MICHAEL: Maybe he'll find some evidence you've over-looked.

LISA: He can't, I've destroyed it all. I destroy it all every day, well I put it in the rubbish bin anyway.

MICHAEL: And what's that? **[Pointing to the rubbish bags]** All your litter from the past six months, what if he tips all that on to the ground?

[DANDILION comes running in.]

DANDI: [To BILLY] I've been looking for you, do you remember me?

BILLY: No.

DANDI: I used to give you free meals . . .

BILLY: I'm sorry I don't really . . .

DANDI: All your friends are in prison.

BILLY: Are they?

DANDI: I saw the police come and take them all away.

BILLY: What did they look like?

DANDI: I don't know, blue uniforms, crash helmets you know.

MICHAEL: His friends he means.

DANDI: There were eight of them carrying instruments, they said they were looking for you.

BILLY: That'll be the band. Last time I saw them they were watching television: they must have come out on tour. What were they arrested for?

DANDI: Killing our chicken.

BILLY: What did they do that for?

DANDI: They didn't.

BILLY: Oh. Who called the police?

DANDI: I did.

BILLY: Oh.

DANDI: I'm really sorry I didn't mean to. I just did what I was told. I might have lost my job. Can't you go and save them? You could be a witness.

BILLY: I don't know where the police station is.

DANDI: I'll show you.

BILLY: Oh.

DANDI: Don't be scared, go and save them.

BILLY: Right.

DANDI: Hurry up, you might be too late.

BILLY: Off I go then . . . what shall I do?

DANDI: Say you're a character witness.

BILLY: OK.

DANDI: You can offer to bail them out.

BILLY: I haven't got any money.

DANDI: Here, I took it from the till.

BILLY: Thanks. Thank you very much.

DANDI: It's the least I can do. Come on.

[The MAN FROM THE COUNCIL comes down the stairs, his pockets bulging and his arms full of LISA's clothes. LISA is following him.]

MAN: Right I'll take this lot as evidence.

LISA: But you can't I'll have nothing to wear.

MAN: Sorry.

LISA: Oh please can't you just leave me a change of underwear?

MAN: Here.

LISA: Thanks. Look I haven't done anything.

MAN: I've told you already. You've been claiming money you're not entitled to. Water rates, gas rates, central heating allowance, you've been claiming all that for three years on top of your rent and there's not a single drop of gas or heating in the place. You'll have to pay it all back. And your rent is much too high. That room isn't worth a fiver! You'll have to pay that back as well. We can't pay rents like that.

LISA: But that's not my fault.

MAN: It certainly isn't my fault. Right let's take a look in these bags shall we?

LISA: No please it's just rubbish, it should have been taken away ages ago.

MAN: Just as well it wasn't then.

[He starts opening the bags and tipping their contents on to the ground. The bags contain nothing but rats.] What's all this then?

33

LISA: Rats.

MAN: I can see that. How come you've got so many?

LISA: They sort of accumulate.

MAN: You can't just dump them here.

LISA: I had to throw them away somewhere.

MAN: Couldn't you throw them down the toilet?

LISA: That's where they came from.

MAN: This is against the by-laws. I'll have to take you in for questioning.

LISA: Oh please it's not my fault.

MAN: Nothing seems to be your fault does it?

LISA: I was just trying to keep the place tidy.

MAN: And what do you think we're going to do with this lot?

LISA: I don't know.

MAN: It costs money to dispose of cadaveric waste you know.

LISA: I'm sorry.

MAN: The council hasn't got enough money as it is.

LISA: I know.

MAN: It's unnecessary expense.

LISA: I'm sorry.

MAN: Someone's going to have to pay for this!

MICHAEL: You can't put all the blame on her, she's just a young girl.

MAN: Still got to take her in.

MICHAEL: What will they do?

MAN: Nothing much. Give her a bit of psychiatric help. Take her baby away from her.

BILLY: I didn't know you had a baby!

LISA: Only a little one, it was premature.

BILLY: Where did it come from?

LISA: Where do you think?

BILLY: I mean . . . I mean whose is it?

LISA: Mine.

BILLY: Yes, but who else's?

LISA: Yours I suppose.

BILLY: Oh. How small is it?

LISA: Very small. It just slipped out.

BILLY: Is it alive?

LISA: Of course it is.

BILLY: What does it do?

LISA: Do? It sleeps.

BILLY: Oh. That's nice.

LISA: It'll do more when it gets older.

BILLY: Yes. Can I go up and see it?

LISA: It's asleep.

MICHAEL: Congratulations.

BILLY: Thank you.

MICHAEL: I wish it was mine.

BILLY: I'm sorry.

MICHAEL: But I'm glad it's yours.

BILLY: Thank you.

MAN: Unfortunately it's no one's. Or more specifically it belongs to the Social Services.

MICHAEL: You can't do that.

MAN: In cases where the mother isn't fit –

MICHAEL: But she is fit.

MAN: She won't be when they put her in prison.

BILLY: It's mine.

MAN: Can't be proved I'm afraid. Where do you live?

BILLY: I live . . . I live erm . . . in various places.

MAN: No fixed abode. No good I'm afraid.

MICHAEL: Actually he was lying, he lives up there with her.

MAN: **[To BILLY]** Oh yes. Tell me, what does the sun god look like?

BILLY: The sun god? I haven't a clue.

MAN: There you can't fool me that easily. He doesn't live up there. He's probably not even the father from what I can see.

LISA: Bloody cheek! I've never been with anyone else.

MAN: Oh yes?

LISA: Not in that way anyway. **[Puts her head on MICHAEL's shoulder.]**

MICHAEL: Don't cry.

MAN: Right come on I've got to get this cleared up somehow.

[PAT comes in accompanied by what looks like a PLAIN-
CLOTHES POLICEMAN. He goes straight up to MUS-
TAFA.]

PAT: There he is!

POLICEMAN: You're under arrest.

MICHAEL: What's going on? Leave him alone.

PAT: You keep quiet.

MICHAEL: So it's you you little worm. What's your
game?

PAT: I'm arresting him. I knew he'd be hiding here.

MICHAEL: He wasn't hiding he was just sitting there.

PAT: That's right, in disguise.

MICHAEL: Can't you dress differently if you want to now?

PAT: And where's his moustache?

MICHAEL: He shaved it off.

PAT: Why?

MICHAEL: It was tickling his nose.

PAT: And what about the glasses?

MICHAEL: They're his reading glasses. He was reading a newspaper, he must have dropped it. Anyway what do you
want him for?

PAT: He broke my window.

MICHAEL: What window?

PAT: My office window. The window to my Party Headquarters. A government office, the nursery of our national
heritage. And what's more he's foreign.

MICHAEL: No he's not.

PAT: What's his name?

MICHAEL: His name? I don't know what his name is. Look
will you shut up and leave us alone, we're occupied on
council business.

DANDI: Mustafa is that you?

MUSTAFA: Hello.

DANDI: I didn't recognize you without your moustache.

MUSTAFA: Do you mind?

DANDI: No, not much. Anyway you can grow it again.

MUSTAFA: What are you doing here?

36

DANDI: Nothing. [To PAT] Your daughter is being taken away did you know?

PAT: She's not my daughter.

DANDI: Well she's being taken away all the same.

PAT: Inevitable.

DANDI: And her baby is being taken away.

PAT: [To the COUNCIL MAN] Excuse me, you know my face I expect, I'm the minister for sanitation and secrecy; that baby up there is mine.

MAN: O K sir that's fine then.

LISA: It's not his it can't be! I've never been anywhere near you!

PAT: Don't you think I ever crawl across from my little bed behind the curtain while you're asleep? Don't you ever have dreams and wonder why? It's difficult to stay pure in the times we live in, conditions are so crowded. Right, let's get moving, take him away.

[MUSTAFA is led away.]

DANDI: Mustafa! Where are they taking you?

MUSTAFA: Not very far away, you can come and visit me.

DANDI: How long will I have to wait?

MUSTAFA: Not very long. Perhaps the next Opening of Parliament might change things, bye bye. [Exits.]

DANDI: Bye bye.

PAT: [To COUNCIL MAN] You'd better take this one away too.

MAN: Certainly Minister. Shall I give you the keys to her flat?

PAT: Thanks.

LISA: My baby!

MAN: Come on now, he's in good hands, he's a government minister that man. Think of the future that baby will have, think of all that heritage.

LISA: My baby! [To MICHAEL and BILLY] Can't you do something, please!

[MICHAEL and BILLY stare at her petrified as she is dragged away.]

PAT: [Takes a deep breath of air.] Ah doesn't the air feel fresh to you. I think it must be spring time soon. It's getting warmer, the snow's beginning to melt off the roofs . . . [**Moves off.**]

MICHAEL: Watch out for falling ice.

[**BILLY clears an area in the rats with his foot and sits down.**]

What are you thinking?

BILLY: I'm hungry.

MICHAEL: What'll we do?

BILLY: We can sit here a while, see what happens.

MICHAEL: And what if nothing happens?

BILLY: We can go away again and then come back. Something's bound to happen eventually isn't it?

MICHAEL: Yes, yes it is.

BILLY: What about him?

MICHAEL: He'll die soon.

BILLY: I hope so.

£   £   £

Ambulance

Characters

JOHNNY	forty
CLIVEY	twenty, black
MARTIN	thirty-seven
ELLIS	thirty-eight, Martin's sister
PEDRO	thirty
TINA	twenty-three
LOUISE	twenty-seven
MARY	twenty-three, black
AMBULANCE CREW	

The action takes place on the street, outside a launderette and also in Ellis's room.

Ambulance was first produced at the Royal Court in September 1987 with the following cast:

JOHNNY	Eamon Boland
CLIVEY	Robbie Gee
MARTIN	Adam Kotz
ELLIS	Patti Love
PEDRO	Kevin McMonagle
TINA	Wendy Nottingham
LOUISE	Julia Swift
MARY	Natasha Williams

Directed by Lindsay Posner
Designed by Anabel Temple
Music by Roland Perrin

ELLIS sitting on the pavement. Drinks down a pint of beer from a glass. Smashes the empty glass on to the pavement, gets up and walks off. Met by PEDRO who fails to get out of her way, they collide then stand staring at one another. Long pause.

PEDRO: Mind where you're going.
[ELLIS mutters drunkenly, pushes past.]
[Stopping her] Tears. Don't just push past. What do you think I am? [Seizes her by her filthy man's jacket.] Having a drink were you? You broke the glass. I bet you're tough aren't you?
[He boxes with her. She stinks. She shies away in horror at being touched. PEDRO holds his arms out to embrace her. She looks up at him. Suddenly he points a finger at her threateningly and holds it there outstretched in front of him, then, just as suddenly, he releases it and his manner becomes friendly again.]
Do you know what my wife told me once? The cosmos is chaos. You know what beauty is? Well there isn't any. You know what wisdom is? There isn't any. And form, there isn't any. Human ideas. Did you ever have an idea? About anything, the stars, for example. The Milky Way. That is an exaggeration. Look at it. I'm on the run, in a way, so are you. We've been too careless. But carelessness is an idea, an exaggeration.
What I'm trying to say to you is, don't cry. Don't worry, it's a kiss. Out of the blackness comes a kiss, and then all of a sudden, you bump your forehead on the moon's crusty surface. Born Again! Life is an extension of death, this is an extension of my arm!
[He holds out his arm, moves closer to her with it, touches her ragged head. She remains still. He opens her shirt and puts his hand inside. She stands for a while as he caresses her, then pulls away in shame.]
It's all right, I was at arm's length from the smell. What's wrong?

43

ELLIS: I can't forgive myself.

PEDRO: Whatever it is forget it.

ELLIS: I have. I don't have any pain.

PEDRO: That's because you're so drunk.

ELLIS: No it isn't.

PEDRO: Well, we can't feel pain all the time, I wouldn't open my mouth. It's all there at the back of your throat, like tonsillitis, you feel it in the morning and then again at night, the day between is just an empty journey from one to the other.

ELLIS: Listen. **[Pulls him closer.]** I'll tell you what, you can forgive a person, anyone, even yourself, but to forgive the person you have to remember the crime. And I can't. I've forgotten what I did.

£   £   £

Outside the launderette. MARTIN, a small withered man in his late thirties. Wears a blue nylon shirt open at the chest revealing twisted and burnt flesh, a red injury reaching to a disfigured ear and hair ill-growing at the side of his tiny skull. He walks stiffly and strangely with his head pulled back, his neck and chin taut. He clutches a white plastic bag to his stomach. His trousers are grey Terylene and stop short of his thin ankles. Short blue socks, moulded shoes. A small bandage around head and ear. He produces a broken pair of binoculars from his plastic bag and puts them to his eyes. Replaces them. Moves on. Stops. A lot of traffic. Lights and noise. MARTIN repeats his movement with binoculars. A girl, TINA, rushes out from the launderette carrying a bundle. She goes straight up to MARTIN.

TINA: I've seen you before. This is my baby. I'm taking it somewhere where it's safe from those washing machines. The fumes are bad for him. Fumes like that can stop a baby breathing, destroy its intelligence, and all its physical reflexes. And the noise can give them a weak heart and make them cry all the time. What's the point of that eh? That's not much of a start in life is it? And it's not just the machines it's the people. They pull him and poke him; try to get his attention. They keep whispering things in his ear. They're trying to twist him, pull him out of shape before he's even human. They want to make him like them. I don't want him to die. I want him to live and be free. I'm going to put him here.

Don't tell anyone.

[She places the baby a little way off behind some cardboard boxes. MARTIN looks off into the darkness through the binoculars. After staring at her baby, TINA goes up to MARTIN.]

What are you looking for?

[MARTIN lowers his binoculars.]

£ £ £

CLIVEY stands alone on crutches. He's nervous but trying to relax. Looks up at the sky. Pause. He hears a noise in some boxes behind him. Turns round with a start.

£ £ £

PEDRO is standing watching MARTIN.

PEDRO: Hey. Let me look through those.

[MARTIN shies away.]

Come on, I'll give them back. [Comes up and takes the binoculars and looks through them.] You can't see anything, it's black. No. It's orange. But you can't see anything. What are you looking for?

[No reply.]

I'll tell you what I'm looking for. An all-night chemist. My children are ill so I've got to get some medicine, quickly. All right. Do you know where one is?

[MARTIN shakes his head.]

45

The thing is, now I've got out of the house I can't bring
myself to go back. Isn't that awful? My wife is nursing the
children, they've got high temperatures. I don't feel too
good myself. It's possible I may never go back. Or I may
go back in a little while.

MARTIN: [Puts his binoculars to his eyes again.] I used
to wear goggles when I swam under water.

PEDRO: Oh yeah? Where was that?

MARTIN: In the sea with the jellyfish.

PEDRO: Right. Good. And now you wear those right?

MARTIN: [Looks at him and smiles.] Yeah!

PEDRO: You look good in them. They go with your scar.

[MARTIN turns away again.]

I noticed it straight away. Disfigured, that's what you are
mate. An industrial accident was it, or were you a baby
and your mummy poured scalding water all over you?
[Pause.]
The world doesn't take care of its weaklings does it?
[Gap. Music. They drink.]

£   £   £

Later. PEDRO is forcing MARTIN to drink from a beer can.

PEDRO: Go on drink it! That's it drink it all down! I want to
see you swallow all this.

[Shakes MARTIN.] Drink!

Come here I want to hug you. [Embraces MARTIN and
hugs him hard to his own body.] Your revolting body!
It's like a fledgling's. Why didn't you grow? I bet your
mother smoked.

[Still hugging him he pulls down MARTIN's shirt and
kisses his massive burn mark, following it down from
his ear to his chest.] Come on! Oo that's lovely.

[PEDRO starts laughing and thrusting his hips towards
MARTIN's groin until MARTIN falls over and PEDRO
falls on top of him. Pause. PEDRO stands up and takes a
few steps away not looking back at MARTIN.]

How am I going to get out of here? Why did you bring me down a road that smells of fish? I could puke. It's everywhere. Look I've been down here a million times before. If I'd wanted to come down here again I would have asked you.

Come on get up.

Look at you, you're like a piece of string. My lips are probably infected. I'm not kissing *you* again. Would you like me to carry you? You look like you could do with a rest.

[Approaches MARTIN, then pushes him away.] Get out. I'm not your bloody mother. You can crawl can't you?

Come on, I want to go now. Be quick. Right. Which way? Right or left? Right or left? Quickly! Left, O K. Hold my hand. And if you run away I'll boot your ankles until they bleed, O K? Martin, Martin you know what you're looking for don't you? All-night chemist. You know that don't you?

[MARTIN starts walking.]

Martin! Martin! **[Stops him.]** Smile!

[They go off.]

£   £   £

LOUISE and CLIVEY.

CLIVEY: I was not with that girl!!

LOUISE: Oh leave me alone Clivey, I can't!

CLIVEY: Come on girl don't be stupid.

LOUISE: **[Seizes his crutch.]** If you say that again I'll brain you with this, I will, I will!

CLIVEY: **[Hopping]** Louise I can't stand up, come on don't be silly.

[LOUISE hits him with his crutch and he falls over.]

Ow Louise my leg! Hey where are you going?! Listen I've tried to be nice to you haven't I?

LOUISE: Get lost!

CLIVEY: You can't just leave me lying here on the pavement like this! Ow it hurts!

LOUISE: Why not? You don't care about me. All you care about is your leg!

CLIVEY: At least help me get on a bus.

LOUISE: A bus!

CLIVEY: A bus. Just a bus!

LOUISE: Where are you going!?

CLIVEY: Nowhere.

LOUISE: You bastard!

CLIVEY: What's the matter with you?

LOUISE: You're going to her! Well you can. I'm going to have a drink, I'm going – [Cries.]

CLIVEY: Louise, it's all right. I won't get a bus. Let's go for a drink, both of us, come on.

LOUISE: No it's not all right! You're so selfish! Everybody says you are. I'm sick of it! I don't think I love you anymore Clivey.

CLIVEY: Listen, this is getting out of hand! You start off saying you don't want me going with other women –

LOUISE: I don't care what you do.

CLIVEY: And now you start laying into me about my personality. What's with all the criticism eh? Is it because I can't stand up? It is isn't it? You'd like me to be always like this wouldn't you? If I was a cripple you'd be puncturing the tyres on my wheelchair.

LOUISE: Listen, are you still my man?

CLIVEY: Come on Louise.

LOUISE: Are you my man?

CLIVEY: Yeah.

LOUISE: Then stop fucking that black whore!

£   £   £

CLIVEY tries to move off, crawling. PEDRO catches sight of him.

PEDRO: Hey Martin, look. It's the Human Spider.

CLIVEY: Did you say to me man?

PEDRO: Hey it speaks.

CLIVEY: Do you want your face busted in half?

PEDRO: Watch it. Martin here has just finished telling me how he used to pull the legs off spiders when he was younger.

CLIVEY: You must be a very careless man to go around talking in that way. But I'm going to let you off if you put me on this bus that's coming along the road now.

PEDRO: You want me and Martin to put you on a bus?

CLIVEY: That's right.

PEDRO: You can't depend on Martin. His mother smoked too much. He sleeps with one eye open and his legs crossed. He can't lift anything, no flesh. You understand?

CLIVEY: You lift me.

PEDRO: All right. Martin, wave your withered limb at this bus. [Lifts CLIVEY.]

£   £   £

TINA wanders about, seems to be looking for something without really looking. JOHNNY keeps his eye on her sensing that she will interfere with him.

JOHNNY: [As TINA approaches] Go away.

TINA: What?

JOHNNY: Go away. I'm having a quiet drink by myself.

TINA: I –

JOHNNY: I'm a man, having a drink.

TINA: I'm looking for my baby.

JOHNNY: What are you asking me for? I can't give you a baby.

TINA: I can't find him anywhere.

JOHNNY: [Seizing her by the scruff of the neck] Look at these eyes. Do I look like a man who's going to give you a baby from somewhere? I'm not going to give you anything. What are you going to give me?

TINA: Let go!

JOHNNY: Are you going to kiss a man like me? You're not going to bother me. [Releases her.]
[TINA resumes her search instantly.]

£   £   £

MARY and CLIVEY in a room. She's kissing him and she's wrapping a bandage around his leg.

CLIVEY: Ow, mind my leg!

MARY: It's twisted around.

CLIVEY: What is?

MARY: This leg.

CLIVEY: What are you, a doctor? I'll do it myself. Listen I've got to get some sleep . . .

MARY: You can't, the woman might come.

CLIVEY: So what?

MARY: What if she throws me out?

CLIVEY: You'll find somewhere else.

MARY: You said you'd find somewhere . . .

CLIVEY: Yeah well . . .

MARY: Come on let me finish your leg. The bandage is dangling.

CLIVEY: Let it dangle.

MARY: You don't care if I go back to prison.

CLIVEY: Come on, I hardly know you.

MARY: I'm not going back to prison because of someone like you.

CLIVEY: This isn't my lucky day.

MARY: I know my legs are going to carry me back to prison. I think it's something they put in the tea. My legs stop all of a sudden as soon as I get out of a certain radius of Holloway . . . I've met so many people like you.

CLIVEY: Well luckily I've never met anyone quite like you before.

£   £   £

TINA **standing still, just about to move off. She sees** MARTIN **and** PEDRO **approaching.**

TINA: Go away.

PEDRO: What?

TINA: Leave me alone.

PEDRO: We've only just got here.

[TINA **moves to go.**]

Are you going to be here long? [**Grabs her.**] Have you got a minute?

TINA: No.

PEDRO: Come on. Don't you want to strike it lucky? You might win something.

TINA: I don't want to win anything, let go.

PEDRO: There are prizes. [**Grabs her by the scruff of the neck.**] Look at me. There are prizes. Don't you want to win a prize?

TINA: No I don't.

PEDRO: I'm not dangerous, you're the dangerous one. Do we look dangerous? We're giving out the prizes.

TINA: [**Pleading**] Please let go of me!

PEDRO: Look, don't get like that. You can have anything. Perfume, a box of tissues, just name it and we'll go and look for it.

Come on. You *do* want something. I can see it in your eyes. And you can see I want to give you something. Can't you? [**Lets go.**]

What's the matter with people these days? They're terrified.

[TINA **runs, bumps into** MARTIN, **runs off.** LOUISE **appears.**]

[**Spins round to** LOUISE] Hey you!

£   £   £

TINA standing alone. In the launderette, all the machines going. The swirling machines are giving out light like televisions. Their noise is music. Music that is washing machines and a clavichord waltz, it twinkles like the stars.

£   £   £

Outside a launderette. Night. JOHNNY comes in with an armful of clothes followed by ELLIS, a woman with a boyish haircut and corduroy trousers with flared bottoms. She carries a plastic beer glass with a pint of beer in it, carefully trying to balance it so that she doesn't spill. She nevertheless is trying to pull JOHNNY back with her other hand.

ELLIS: Come on Johnny where are you going?

JOHNNY: Here. I told you. Leave off.

ELLIS: No but what for?

JOHNNY: Stop pulling my jumper you'll stretch it.

ELLIS: Come on Johnny.

JOHNNY: I'm going here all right?

ELLIS: Don't you love me any more Johnny? [Tries to hug him.]

JOHNNY: Put me down you've spilled your beer.

ELLIS: What's a bit of spilt beer . . .

JOHNNY: Bloody mess . . .

ELLIS: I've made the pavement dirty! Wait a minute I'll lick it up. Hold my beer please while I put my tongue on the floor.

JOHNNY: Don't be dirty woman.

ELLIS: Come on Johnny, come down here with me and have a lick yourself.

JOHNNY: I want a young woman.

ELLIS: I am young. I'm twenty-six, thirty-six years old.

JOHNNY: You're too old, get up.

ELLIS: I'm twenty-six you bastard, come on.

JOHNNY: I need a young girl otherwise I'm useless.

ELLIS: What do you mean, isn't twenty-six young enough for you?

JOHNNY: Eighteen.

ELLIS: Oh you rotten bastard, you rotten bastard! **[Kicks at him from the ground.]**

JOHNNY: I don't like your wrinkles. You're wrinkled all over, it makes me feel sick, come on get up.

ELLIS: Urgh I've wet myself!

JOHNNY: Oh you filthy cow get up!

ELLIS: Urggh! **[Cries.]**

JOHNNY: You piece of shite. Go away from me. I'll never get anywhere if you keep pissing yourself.

ELLIS: Help me!

JOHNNY: No, no step back, you'll make me smell.

ELLIS: It's all wet!

JOHNNY: **[Sniffs.]** It's beer you stupid bitch. You sat in your beer!

ELLIS: Oh! Oh! **[Shrieks with laughter.]** I sat in my beer! I thought I'd pissed myself. Whoo hoo!

JOHNNY: You're still wet anyway.

ELLIS: Are you thirsty?

[JOHNNY hands her back the beer and turns to the door of the launderette which is closed. The lights are out except a night light.]

JOHNNY: Open up!

ELLIS: I'm going to finish this off now so if you want a drink later you'll have to suck my trousers.

JOHNNY: What's the matter with them!

ELLIS: They're closed.

JOHNNY: Open this door!

ELLIS: They've gone to bed exhausted. It's all that scrubbing. It tires them out.

JOHNNY: They don't scrub, they have machines.

ELLIS: What?

JOHNNY: Machines. To do the washing.

ELLIS: Eh?

JOHNNY: Washing machines.

ELLIS: Bugger me.

JOHNNY: Obviously you've never been.

ELLIS: What? Here? I come here every day.

JOHNNY: You must have seen the machines then.

ELLIS: Of course I have. I just didn't know what they were for.

JOHNNY: What do you do here then?

ELLIS: Try on clothes.

JOHNNY: [Rattles door.] Open this launderette! I want to wash my clothes.

ELLIS: Don't worry about your clothes Johnny, nobody cares about that. It's the inner man . . .

JOHNNY: People want to see clean shirts.

[JOHNNY starts thumping on the door. A voice from inside, 'All right, all right', the door is unlocked.]

TINA: We're closed – MY BABY!

[TINA rushes out and seizes JOHNNY's bundle of clothes.]

You've found him!

JOHNNY: No, no.

TINA: My baby!

JOHNNY: My clothes!

TINA: Give him to me!

JOHNNY: Stop pulling. This isn't your baby!

TINA: Let me see.

JOHNNY: Look, clothes see.

TINA: Where's my baby then?

JOHNNY: I don't know.

TINA: [To ELLIS] Do you know this man took my baby from its pram, I was in a sweet shop. And now he won't give it back.

JOHNNY: These are just my clothes, I want to wash them.

TINA: And what about my baby's clothes, aren't you going to wash them?

JOHNNY: I haven't got your baby.

TINA: Yes you have.

JOHNNY: Will you wash these or not?

TINA: All right. Wait a minute. [Turns to ELLIS.] Have you seen my baby? This man is probably protecting some-

one, a young woman I reckon, just like me, but sad, you
know what I mean? She must have been desperate. A bit
mad. I forgive her but I want my baby back. Can you wait?

JOHNNY: What for?

TINA: They're so dirty. [To ELLIS] Men are always full of
dirt aren't they?

[ELLIS steps back shyly. TINA is made suspicious. She
points her finger from one to the other, her eyes ablaze.]
You! You two are in it together. *You* stole my baby!

ELLIS: Leave off! I didn't steal your baby.

TINA: You did. You did! Why?! Oh please, please give him
back to me. Please. You don't understand. He is mine.
I'm his mother. You can't keep him.

ELLIS: Listen I haven't got him. I haven't even seen a baby for
nineteen years so leave me alone.

JOHNNY: [To TINA] Look you'd better go and put those in a
machine or we'll be here all night.

TINA: I can't. I haven't got a basket.

JOHNNY: I'll get you one. [Goes in.]

[TINA stands waiting holding the bundle of clothes
to her breast.]

ELLIS: Here, have some of this.

TINA: You don't know what it's like to be a mother. I look
young to you don't I? I'm not really. I'm old. Older than
you. My baby used to suck at my breasts. This isn't my
baby. This is a bundle of clothes.

[JOHNNY comes with a basket. She dumps the bundle
into the basket and goes.]

ELLIS: [Slumps against the wall, tired.] Right. Where's
she gone then?

JOHNNY: She's washing my clothes I hope.

ELLIS: She could have asked us in for a warm.

JOHNNY: A warm? It's not warm in there. It's the wind from
those driers, they seem to get it from another universe.

ELLIS: I'm cold Johnny.

£   £   £

55

PEDRO, MARTIN and LOUISE (sitting).

PEDRO: Martin, this girl has lost her boyfriend – you see what happens if you go looking too hard for things.

LOUISE: Stop talking will ya.

PEDRO: Here, let me wipe all that make-up off your face.

LOUISE: Leave off!

PEDRO: I can't be your lover. I wish I could. I've got one. She's waiting for me. She's a mathematician.

I prefer friendship. I only wish Martin here was up to it. Listen, don't just sit there looking pissed off. Why don't you go home or something?

LOUISE: I'm not going back until he's there.

£   £   £

JOHNNY and ELLIS still outside the launderette.

ELLIS: You know if you were to let me come home with you I'd make you a good home for you to be comfortable in . . .

You're such a fine man with your intelligence and your dreams, and what with me with my, with my . . . with my being a woman. We'd have a lovely time Johnny.

JOHNNY: Please don't, you'll stir painful memories.

ELLIS: What painful memories?

JOHNNY: I recall . . . I was sitting upstairs, the newspaper spread across my knees at the top of the house, and from down below where we had the bathroom I heard the sounds of my wife and my small daughter bathing together. The noise of the gentle splashing drifted up to me in my solitude and my daughter laughing and laughing and laughing until she sounded as if she was in pain, and her little voice, 'Mamma, mamma, mamma.' [Pause.] And now they are both gone.

ELLIS: Johnny you're lying. You were never married. You have no daughter!

JOHNNY: [Sighs.] Yes you're right. But does that make the pain of separation any easier to bear?

56

ELLIS: The fact is you are afraid of women. I think you are a
bit scared of the meaty side of it, if you see what I mean.
Women as you probably know are not like men, they are
meatier. And I think it's that that bothers you. We –

JOHNNY: Please –

ELLIS: No I think I know what it is. It's because we're a bit
like that meat you see hanging up in the butcher's, because
you can stick your hand up inside of us and ruck it around
and I suppose it feels a bit like when you're wrestling with
that joint to get it into the oven.

JOHNNY: I wouldn't know.

£ £ £

**A clavichord waltz. Music that twinkles like the
stars.**

PEDRO: **[Shaking his head as if to clear it.]** Listen to
that. I can't hear anything. Do you know I knew someone
who used to clean out my ears for me.

Look I'm going deaf. It sounds like winter but it looks
like summer.

I'm going to have to leave you soon. Martin and I have
got an appointment. There's this midget you see who
promised Martin to tell him his fortune. Only he's in
prison. So we're going to wait outside by the wall.

You can't come. You live around here don't you? So you
can't. This is a mystery. We don't want the local residents
interfering.

[LOUISE drinks.]

Stop that! Just for a moment can't you! Always the same
bloody thing. Haven't you got any curiosity? I suppose
you're going to sleep with your face in a bucket. You
probably haven't even got a fortune. That's it. No
wonder you're not interested. You stay here, we'll go on
alone.

**[LOUISE struggles to her feet and moves off in the other
direction.]**

57

[Goes after her.] Come on, you're not off to lover boy are you?

[LOUISE keeps going.]

He's too good for you! Come back!

There goes another one. The girls around here are like falling stars.

£   £   £

ELLIS and JOHNNY outside the launderette.

ELLIS: So ... I may be dirty and smelly on the outside, but once you get inside, I promise you I'm as fresh as a baby.

JOHNNY: Look stop this!

£   £   £

The time is broken by slow music. PEDRO and MARTIN standing apart.

PEDRO: **[Flicks up his eyes to the firmament.]**

Look out Martin, look out!

[Flicks up his eyes again and smiles.]

£   £   £

ELLIS and JOHNNY outside the launderette.

JOHNNY: Anyway, I'm not as inexperienced as you think, in fact I'm having an affair with her.

ELLIS: Who?

JOHNNY: That girl in there.

ELLIS: What? Her?

JOHNNY: You heard what she said.

ELLIS: What?

JOHNNY: She said I'd taken her baby. Well I have. It's our baby. I'm the father. I've taken it away because I don't think she's fit to look after it properly. No, no you see, she couldn't educate it with books like I could.

ELLIS: Where is it then?

JOHNNY: Where is it?

ELLIS: Yeah where is it?

JOHNNY: At home.

ELLIS: What, on its own?

JOHNNY: No, no. The ambulance came and took it away. It wasn't well.

ELLIS: Oh.

JOHNNY: Yes they said she'd beaten it and they'd bring it back to me when it was better.

ELLIS: It's your child?

JOHNNY: Yes.

ELLIS: How?

JOHNNY: Eh?

ELLIS: How come?

JOHNNY: I kept coming here. Lots of things go on in here you know. Dances, parties. At night when you are out wandering around too drunk to notice.

ELLIS: No it's not true!

JOHNNY: Oh yes. Oh I've had some good times here. Lots of pretty girls used to come, and all sorts of people. Anyway she and I got acquainted.

ELLIS: [Angry] What do you mean acquainted?

JOHNNY: Yes, she thought I was interesting. Interesting and handsome. Well anyway you know what it's like at parties, lots of kissing and that kind of thing.

ELLIS: Did she kiss *you*?

JOHNNY: Oh yes, not just me. But mostly me.

ELLIS: Ha, that doesn't make babies you know!

JOHNNY: No. We did it.

ELLIS: Where?

JOHNNY: Behind the washing machines.

ELLIS: You filthy bastard. It's not true, you're not capable.

JOHNNY: It's true! And actually it's one reason why I can't allow you to come home with me.

ELLIS: What do you mean?

JOHNNY: I have to create the right sort of moral environment for the child.

ELLIS: I'm not moral enough am I?

JOHNNY: It's not that. It's just that the young mind is impressionable. I don't want it to think I run around with lots of different women . . .

£ £ £

MARTIN and PEDRO. A puff of smoke suddenly goes up from behind. PEDRO starts. Puts his arms around MARTIN to protect him.

MARTIN: What was that?

PEDRO: Don't worry Martin. It was just a puff of smoke from behind that petrol station. Look, it's all gone now. It wasn't anything, just some old boxes going up, that's all. Just a false wind. Just a false wind. It's gone now.

£ £ £

Outside the launderette. ELLIS has her head in her hands.

ELLIS: I've got to have a piss. Where can I go? My legs won't carry me. Why's that eh? You tell me Johnny if you're so clever.

JOHNNY: I'll help you, come on.

ELLIS: No it's all right I can crawl.

[LOUISE comes in. ELLIS arrives at LOUISE's feet.]
Oh god.

[ELLIS gets up stumbles over to some cardboard boxes behind. LOUISE stares at her. JOHNNY goes to LOUISE.]

LOUISE: I'm sick of it Johnny, I'm sick of it.

JOHNNY: Are you? Come and have a few laughs with me.

LOUISE: He doesn't care.

JOHNNY: Doesn't he? That's terrible.

ELLIS: There's a baby behind here.

LOUISE: Do you know how he got his leg busted?

JOHNNY: No, no I don't.

60

LOUISE: Neither does he. He just woke up like it one morning.

ELLIS: **[From behind]** It's wrapped up in a paper bag.

LOUISE: What if it spreads to the rest of his body? I might have to nurse him until he dies a twisted death.

JOHNNY: Ellis has been making up stories about me. She's accusing me of having sex in a launderette. She said there were wild parties there.

LOUISE: Did she?

JOHNNY: In here she means, right here. But really all I ever do is get my clothes washed. That's what I'm doing now.

LOUISE: **[Drinks, pause.]** Where's Ellis?

JOHNNY: She ran off.

£   £   £

ELLIS's room where MARY and CLIVEY are asleep. Electric music, orangey lights from outside and a chip shop sign flashes on and off occasionally. A radio is playing in another part of the building. The window is open. Traffic noises filter up from the street. Below a man is singing 'When you're in love' over and over again.

ELLIS stumbles into the room carrying a bundle that is a baby.

ELLIS: Yes we're going home now. We're home. Isn't that nice eh? After all this time.

We'll warm you up in here. Nice and gently. I won't ask where you've been all this time because I don't want you to shock me.

But you mustn't ask me where I've been. I haven't been anywhere. No, I promise you. Nowhere at all in all these years. I haven't taken three steps in one direction or the other. I couldn't, in case you came back. I had to stay here. And I haven't done anything, I've just been passing the time.

But it's all over now.

We'll have a new beginning won't we love? Together.

61

[Rocks the baby to her chest.]

What's that bloody racket?

[Runs to the window.]

What's that bloody racket!

['When you're in love']

How can a baby sleep? Quiet down there!

[CLIVEY rolls over in his sleep.]

I'd put you in bed but that girl is there. I'll turn her out don't worry. I won't let her near you. She'll want you all for herself.

[The music from the radio in another part of the building begins to get louder and louder during the following speech so that ELLIS is screaming the words.]

I knew this was going to happen. Do you know what happened the other day? I was looking for something amongst some cardboard boxes someone had left on the pavement and suddenly this dwarf jumped up out of all the rubbish and ran off down the road. He had tiny fat legs and an enormous fat head. He looked like a baby, he'd been asleep. I thought it was you.

I thought it was you my little sweetheart.

How can I get out of here?

You see, I keep thinking of all the damage you do to your children. You know, I would have done more harm to you if I hadn't deserted you. I'm such a terrible one. *He* was always telling me that. He was right.

Look at the place. I'm so untidy, I can never remember anything, and I eat rubbish. And I've got such a fierce temper. How I would have shouted at you. My eyes are rat's eyes. Rat's eyes.

Look at the way I'm holding you now. All tight and cruel. Fingers like traps.

I'd better put you down, right now. Yes, right now. **[Puts him down.]**

You would have been horrified if you'd seen me like I am now. It's horrible. Would you like to see?

[Stands in front of a mirror.]

62

My eyes are rats and they nibble at you while you are asleep.

He always said that. But it's not his fault. He was on the run; when we had – we did it by the seaside, on a stone. My legs felt like rock afterwards.

He was, he was ... oh he was hardly alive he was so scared of being caught and taken back. He said he was trying to stay alive long enough to make it across the Channel in one of those boats.

'Wait for my night to come,' he said. 'Wait for my night to come.' I don't know what he meant. Then he squeezed my breasts, he squeezed too hard and it hurt because he was a desperate boy he was. 'Watch the stars,' he said. 'Hold on and watch the stars.' And the stars jiggered about and I watched. His skin was black and his eyes were as big and brown as these. **[Fingers her nipples then holds her sagging breasts.]**

Now look at them! They were volcanoes, now they've blown up and fallen down and everything else fell down with them.

Look at them!

All that melted mud on my belly in a sack. All the dead bodies.

[Tears.] 'You're going to see the world,' I said. 'I'd rather see your body,' he said.

[She drops her trousers quickly and desperately. She wears a dirty pair of men's underpants.]

Look, look all the walls have caved in. My belly button's gone as well. The world went down the plughole and filled it in. **[In tears]** The world's gone down the bloody plughole!

[She remains standing in front of the mirror. The music has reached its loudest and the volume drops again. MARY has woken up and walked across the floor to ELLIS. Her young body is a strong contrast to ELLIS's worn-out one.]

MARY: **[Gently]** What's wrong woman?

63

[The two women stand facing each other.]

ELLIS: You step back in time and you find your whole life has been a nightmare.

MARY: What's that on the floor?

ELLIS: A baby.

MARY: Where did you get it?

ELLIS: I lost it and then I found it.

MARY: Where?

ELLIS: It's funny, I didn't remember leaving it there.

[CLIVEY, awake, comes over.]

CLIVEY: What's going on?

[ELLIS, shamed, pulls her clothes on awkwardly.]

MARY: She's stolen a baby.

ELLIS: I did not steal it, it's mine. **[Gently]** Who is he?

MARY: A friend of mine. How did you lose it?

ELLIS: **[Looks at CLIVEY]** It's not my fault. I was very young. No one helped me. I just put it down and when I turned around it was gone. I never thought he would turn up. It's funny how things turn out isn't it?

CLIVEY: This must have been some time ago, right?

ELLIS: Twenty years.

CLIVEY: Twenty years.

[MARY and CLIVEY look towards the baby. Pause.]
Time flies.

[Pause.]
Well, I reckon we'd best be going, it's getting late, nearly time to get up I mean, and er ... hey Mary would you hand me my crutch?

MARY: We can't just go!

CLIVEY: Why not?

MARY: This baby.

CLIVEY: It's not yours is it?

MARY: No but ...

CLIVEY: Well then, you see I prefer to mind my own business.

MARY: Listen woman, this isn't a sack of potatoes, this is an infant you know. What are you going to do with it?

ELLIS: Don't start telling me. I'm a mother, I've been a mother longer than you've been able to walk.

MARY: You're sick, you ought to be in the hospital.

ELLIS: You ought to be back in prison.

MARY: That baby is very young. Give it to me. I can feed it.

ELLIS: No.

MARY: Can you feed it?

ELLIS: It's not hungry.

MARY: It's half dead.

ELLIS: It's having a rest. Don't please –

MARY: You don't know nothing.

ELLIS: Please I'll remember.

MARY: What have you got in your tits old woman? I've still got milk, you've got lager. Hand it over.

ELLIS: You haven't got milk.

MARY: They took my baby away because I bit the ear off a prison warder. I've been squirting it down your sink.

ELLIS: I don't want to lose my little boy again. I want to see if he recognizes me when he wakes up.

CLIVEY: You've probably changed a bit in the last twenty years, you might have to jog his memory.

ELLIS: He used to say mummummumum, mum.

CLIVEY: And what did you say?

ELLIS: I said, 'Where's your dad?'

CLIVEY: And what did he say?

ELLIS: In the pub. Dead at the bottom of the sea. Lying with his head in a dustbin somewhere, crushed, just like he crushed me.

CLIVEY: And then your baby just disappeared?

ELLIS: Someone walked off with him. She was probably not right in the head, the one that did it, but I forgive her. Or sane one minute and mad the next, that's probably what she was, the one that took him. She's probably sitting alone somewhere now behind a curtain with her tights hanging over the oven, wondering where her stolen baby boy has got to. She needn't worry.

MARY: Give him to me now.

ELLIS: I don't think he's warm enough. [Hands him over.]

MARY: He's cold . . .

ELLIS: You can't trust other people to look after your baby. And who ever helped anyone they didn't know to stay warm? Where's your baby?

MARY: In prison.

ELLIS: Yes, they lock them up young nowadays, stealing the milk probably, the little ones are devils for the milk. Are you going to give my son some of yours?

MARY: He won't wake up.

ELLIS: Yes, they're devils for the sleep as well. Shake him a little, gently. My mother used to shake me. And if we got wet she'd hang us over the oven to dry.

[MARY starts crying silently.]

Of course no amount of heat is going to keep a child happy. My mum was a bit over-anxious about the heat since it was never warm enough and we were always shivering. But she shouldn't have concentrated so much on it. I mean it's warm enough in here isn't it? It's summer. But that doesn't seem to keep him happy does it? He's cold anyway isn't he?

[MARY sobs.]

CLIVEY: What's going on?

MARY: It's dead.

CLIVEY: What?

MARY: The baby.

ELLIS: No amount of heat will keep him warm. He's stone cold isn't he?

MARY: Yes.

ELLIS: Whereas I think it's warm in here. Too warm. But he doesn't you see. People are different. [Goes to the window.] Why? What makes it so hot in here? It's like an oven. I'd rather be out there. [Climbs to the window.]

£   £   £

A road, dark, orangey light, dark wind, cold ears, thin traffic PEDRO and MARTIN lumber along. PEDRO walking behind with stronger steps but his pace is hampered by a spasm which contorts his body. The essential of this spasm is a sweeping movement of the arm to the side and behind as if pushing something back that persistently approaches him from over his shoulder. 'Get back,' he mutters.

PEDRO: Wait. Do you know where we are?

> [MARTIN stops but keeps his head facing forwards. Pause. PEDRO's spasm.]

> Wait. [Another spasm.] Do you know where we are? Eh? Martin, speak to me.

MARTIN: I had a bottle with shells in. He said it would cure me.

PEDRO: Come on Martin please ... Do you remember what we're looking for? You don't know how a father suffers. Just out having a good time while my wife nurses our sick children, that's what you think. How would you know? You've taken me on a wild fucking goose chase.

MARTIN: The bottle broke on the beach. I looked for my shells but there were too many.

PEDRO: I'll tell you, if we don't get the medicine soon they'll die, how about that? Nothing impresses you does it?

> [MARTIN gets out a small bottle of spirit and drinks.]

> Where did you get that? You didn't show me that!

MARTIN: Eh?

PEDRO: *Where did you get it?*

MARTIN: My sister. [Hands it to PEDRO.]

PEDRO: Eh? [Laughs.] Your what? [Drinks.]

> [MARTIN laughs in return.]

> You've got a sister?

> [MARTIN laughs some more, enthusiastically.]

> Why didn't you tell me about that, eh?

> [MARTIN continues trying to laugh.]

> Stop bloody laughing!

MARTIN: I've got a sister. [Tries to laugh.]

PEDRO: All right. It's not funny any more. Where is she?

MARTIN: Here.

PEDRO: Where?

MARTIN: Here.

PEDRO: Keeps you happy does she?

MARTIN: Eh?

PEDRO: Your sister. Gives you booze, keeps you happy?

MARTIN: Yeah. [Nods, smiles.]

PEDRO: Why don't you take me to your sister? Why not eh? She on the bottle is she?

MARTIN: Yeah.

PEDRO: I bet she's a pretty sight.

MARTIN: Yeah.

PEDRO: Martin.

MARTIN: Mh?

PEDRO: Don't be stupid now, pay attention when I'm talking to you. [Spasm.] She make you like this?

MARTIN: No.

PEDRO: You are a weakling Martin. I won't let them touch you. Of course I might sell you. Wouldn't get much though because you couldn't do a good day's work could you? When did you last lift a finger to help yourself or anyone else? You have no sense of responsibility. You wander around like a ballerina. [Spasm.] Your life is a pirouette. [Spasm.] What have you done to me?

[Utters three noises, hums, on the same note, a nervous sound, involuntary.]

Voices.

[Starts to cry for one second, stops.]

Martin, I want to meet your sister.

I want to MEAT your sister, do you know what that means? I want to raise a finger to help her. [Makes a gesture with his middle finger.] I'm vulgar, I'm desperate. I'm the modern voice amongst the left-behinds.

Listen, why don't you tell me about somewhere nice? There must be somewhere you'd like to be eh? There is isn't there?

68

[MARTIN **looks at** PEDRO **with a worried frown.**]
[**Puts his arm around** MARTIN'**s shoulders.**] Come
on Martin. I'm all right. I'm the nearest thing to a friend
you'll ever get. I like secrets. I can keep them.
[MARTIN **offers** PEDRO **the bottle.**]
[**Takes bottle.**] This is the longest night of my life.
[**Hands it back.**] Your saliva is very sticky. I noticed it
around the lip of the neck of the bottle you just gave me.
And now I think about it you have little deposits of froth
at the corners of your mouth. That's how we can all be
sure you're not a baby, Martin. Babies don't drink or get
dry. Do you know they take the brain cells from failed
foetuses to heal the ailing skulls of the old? Watch out
Martin. If you can't stop smiling like a foetus in a sink
someone's going to make a long life out of you.

MARTIN: I stood on a piece of grass.

PEDRO: A piece of grass, by the kerbside was it?

MARTIN: ?

PEDRO: A piece of grass. Where the doggies go.

MARTIN: No.

PEDRO: Oh. Good. All right, come on.

MARTIN: A big road.

PEDRO: That's what I said.

MARTIN: Really big.

PEDRO: So you like motorways.

MARTIN: Yes.

PEDRO: Is there any more?

MARTIN: Mm?

PEDRO: Well what happened?

MARTIN: Nothing.

PEDRO: Nothing.

MARTIN: I like big roads, you can see the stars.

PEDRO: Oh yeah. [**Spasm. Notices a lump on the
ground.**] What's that?

MARTIN: My sister.

PEDRO: I should have expected it. She's a mess Martin. Listen
I didn't escape home and family for this . . . or did I? No,

I didn't. My children lay dying. No, coughing, sweating, sneezing. They're probably delirious. And you just take me further away, further away. [Looks at ELLIS.] She's got an honest face. So have we all. All honest faces. Smile Martin. [Spasm.]

She's waiting for me now. Her face at the window. Counting the footfalls of all the ragged men going past our door stealing the milk. Maybe she'll throw herself out to them like a mad penguin into the icy sea. Or she might throw the babies out. So what's the matter with her [ELLIS] then? Eh Martin?

MARTIN: She's resting.

PEDRO: And why is she resting?

MARTIN: Because her head is bleeding.

PEDRO: Is it? [Looks.] And why is her head bleeding?

MARTIN: Because she hit it on the ground.

PEDRO: Why did she hit it on the ground?

MARTIN: She was angry.

PEDRO: Really? No come on I bet she's not like that.

[MARTIN gets out his binoculars.]

I said I bet she's not like that! Martin.

[MARTIN looks into the distance through binoculars.]

You can't hide from it. Your sister lies bleeding at your feet. This isn't the first time. [Spasm.] And it isn't the last.

Where's the treasure eh?

[MARTIN – binoculars.]

Slumped sisters, blood on the paving stones. Binoculars. Where's the treasure chest?

MARTIN: There isn't any.

PEDRO: Can't you ... [Spasm.] Can't you find it by the stars or something? [Grabs him.] Well go on, look! I didn't just come out here for a piss. For a walk in the warm wonderful air to shake my willy did I? [Shouts] What have you got Martin!

[MARTIN grasps his binoculars very tightly.]

You're right. There's no reason to lose my brain. I want

to get on with people, but I am trying to learn to insist on my own terms. I've had more fights in the past weeks . . . But otherwise I'd fade away. I want to look these people in the eye. Come on let's pick her up.

MARTIN: No.

PEDRO: Eh? You're right. Why pick her up? She's resting.

People interfere because they want to take her soul home in their wallet.

Don't they? I'll keep them off. I'll hold them back . . . I'll lay down my body before the battering ram, and jam up the wheels, I'll do that for you Martin.

What's the matter Martin? You're crying. Real tears. Real tears. [Dries them gently with his fingers.] Martin, poor Martin. Look, I'll stroke her head. Like this.

MARTIN: She's cold.

[PEDRO takes off his jacket and puts it over her. He strokes her hair softly. MARTIN starts sobbing violently. PEDRO goes to him.]

PEDRO: Memories. Is it memories?

MARTIN: She fell off the oven. She tried to save me. Her feet got burnt. They smoked. Her blood was on the kitchen floor.

PEDRO: Your mother smoked you too much didn't she?

MARTIN: She tried to keep us warm.

PEDRO: She's still breathing anyway, she isn't dead.

[MARTIN returns the binoculars to his eyes.]

She isn't dead. That's something. [Spasm.] Isn't it Martin? Your sister is still alive and kicking.

We can stand on guard in case someone comes along and starts kicking her. They might try and sweep her up or something, eh? Put her in the trash can where she belongs, eh Martin? We'll put a stop to that. Life goes on. Doesn't it? We don't flinch.

[Ambulance music, sirens, very loud engine noise, screeching of brakes, slamming of doors, croaking babble of radio. The ambulance has arrived. The ambulance crew come on. Played by the same actors as

71

JOHNNY and LOUISE, in smart grey uniforms. PEDRO pushes MARTIN in front of ELLIS to hide her.]

AMBULANCEMAN: Good evening sir.

PEDRO: Good evening.

AMBULANCEMAN: Everything all right is it?

PEDRO: Terrific.

AMBULANCEWOMAN: We've had reports of a body in the neighbourhood.

PEDRO: Ah.

AMBULANCEMAN: Yes. Have you seen one?

PEDRO: No, but I'll ask my friend if you like.

AMBULANCEWOMAN: We can do that thanks. [Goes to MARTIN.] Good evening sir.

[No reply.]

We've had reports of a person lying on the pavement. Have you seen anyone?

[MARTIN puts his binoculars to his eyes.]

It's all right, don't bother looking for it now. Did you see anyone before?

[MARTIN points at PEDRO.]

He was lying down was he?

[MARTIN nods.]

AMBULANCEMAN: Is that right sir? Were you lying down here?

PEDRO: Yes that's right.

AMBULANCEMAN: What for sir?

PEDRO: What for? Well you can't stay upright all the time, you'd end up falling over.

AMBULANCEWOMAN: I'm sorry, I didn't get that? [Gets notebook out.]

PEDRO: Listen, I don't want to keep you unnecessarily from your duties.

AMBULANCEMAN: You're not.

PEDRO: Oh.

AMBULANCEWOMAN: So what was it you said?

PEDRO: I said there's nothing to worry about, we're OK.

AMBULANCEWOMAN: Who is?

72

PEDRO: Me and Martin.

AMBULANCEMAN: Well we got called out to collect an unconscious body on the pavement. So we've got to get one, do you understand?

AMBULANCEWOMAN: We're not going back empty-handed.

AMBULANCEMAN: That's right. Now we're going to drive round a bit and see if we can spot anything.

AMBULANCEWOMAN: And if we don't spot anything we're coming straight back.

AMBULANCEMAN: All right?

AMBULANCEWOMAN: All right he said!

PEDRO: Yes that's fine.

AMBULANCEWOMAN: Listen we're not just out driving around for our own pleasure.

PEDRO: No.

AMBULANCEWOMAN: Denny, I don't like this geezer. He's sick.

AMBULANCEMAN: You've got to start getting used to them Lis [Lisa].

AMBULANCEWOMAN: He makes my fingers itch. He makes me want to get the stretcher out, know what I mean?

AMBULANCEMAN: I know exactly what you mean.

AMBULANCEWOMAN: I mean a transfusion or something.

AMBULANCEMAN: I know, I know, I was thinking exactly the same thing.

AMBULANCEWOMAN: I mean I want to start serving the public. Helping them. And this geezer, and this one, they need cleaning up. You know what I mean?

AMBULANCEMAN: All right Lis. We'll be back all right!

[AMBULANCEWOMAN pockets notebook. Points finger at PEDRO. They go. Ambulance noise and lights move away.]

PEDRO: Well are we all still here? Look at her [Ellis]. Does she look like someone you can save? Eh? [Spasm.] [MARY comes in carrying a large box carefully tied up with bits of string. CLIVEY follows on his crutches.] Ah it's you. I thought I heard giant's footsteps.

CLIVEY: I'm warning you!

[MARTIN regards CLIVEY with his binoculars, CLIVEY stares back so MARTIN looks away.]

PEDRO: Martin, look! There's the treasure we've been searching for all night. The chest. Just think, we can cart it round with us where ever we go. Hand it over.

MARY: You're mad, let go!

CLIVEY: Let go of that box you fucking nutter.

PEDRO: The Human Spider! You can't stand in the way of this. A box is a box. Martin and I are determined.

[He pushes CLIVEY to the floor. CLIVEY lies on his back staring up at the sky, wordless.]

MARY: No, you can't! There's a baby inside it!

PEDRO: A baby? Hear that Martin? What greater treasure could we have hoped to find? A human being with all its future ahead of it!

MARY: It's dead.

PEDRO: Dead? It will have to do. Hand it over.

MARY: [Gives it to him.] Take it then. I don't care. This woman had it. [Indicates ELLIS.]

PEDRO: Did she?

MARY: She must have dropped it or something.

PEDRO: Probably. These things happen. Did you make this box up?

MARY: Yes.

PEDRO: Why?

MARY: It had to be hidden somehow.

PEDRO: Don't worry.

MARY: I didn't kill it.

PEDRO: Good.

MARY: Nobody did. I've got a baby of my own.

[PEDRO dries her eyes with his fingers.]

I was in the middle of feeding it when they took it away from me. I'm going back to the prison now to look for it.

PEDRO: Prison. You won't find it there. They've given it to some Nice People by now. When you get there, look in the car park.

MARY: What if I never find it?

PEDRO: Martin here could do with the milk. A life for a life, it's the same thing. He's only a child.

[A blue light goes by silently. Everything freezes in the blue haze. MARY scurries away.]

Look Martin, look what we've got here. **[Spasm.]** Do you think we'll get away with it? Look at these people, they're our friends. But between us all we've dropped this bouncing baby on the floor, we couldn't cope with it. We didn't have the equipment, not between us. And now it's dead.

[MARTIN puts his binoculars to his eyes.]

We'd better run. They'll get us. They're bound to get us for this. It's hopeless after all isn't it?

[MARTIN just carries on looking through his binoculars. The music we've been hearing from a window up above gets louder and trafficky: out of the traffic sounds emerges the hooting and screeching of tyres and revving of engines, shouts of angry drivers. Enter JOHNNY and LOUISE escaping being run over.]

JOHNNY: **[His arm around LOUISE's shoulder and guiding her to the kerb]** Mind the cars, oops mind the cars mind the cars. Now, I quite agree with what you said just now: strength of mind is often in the legs.

LOUISE: Did I say that?

JOHNNY: The ability to walk, to go in the opposite direction. Now you've got strong white legs, if you could train them to take you in the other direction you'd be happy.

LOUISE: Are *you* happy?

JOHNNY: Am I happy?

LOUISE: Yes.

JOHNNY: Would you like to see my legs?

LOUISE: No I don't!

JOHNNY: No, come on I'll show them to you.

LOUISE: I want to sit down.

JOHNNY: Sit down? No! Keep moving! Now I'll be on the move until my washing is done then hopefully I will

change into my dancing clothes and go on to a club somewhere. **[Shouts]** Keep moving!

LOUISE: Clivey!

JOHNNY: No, keep –

LOUISE: There you are!

JOHNNY: My legs are white, like yours but thin. Bones. Like
my eyes. Do you look in the mirror?

LOUISE: Where the fucking hell have you been?

JOHNNY: I'm sure you do. And what do you see there? All the
way down and all the way up. That's not what I see. I see
my bone eyes, my dreams. Can you smile? **[Pulls her
round and makes her listen.]**

LOUISE: Course I fuckin' can!

JOHNNY: But in the mirror? Can you smile into the mirror at
yourself, into your pavement eyes?

LOUISE: Leave off will ya – Clivey –

CLIVEY: You just left me on the floor, my legs got worse.

JOHNNY: Eyes of Scottish concrete.

LOUISE: But so have mine, I've started limping.

CLIVEY: Why's that then?

LOUISE: I think it's because you go with other girls.

JOHNNY: They roll the roads at this time of night with little
stones to make it easier for us all to tumble down to the
bottom of the hills by daybreak.

CLIVEY: That doesn't give you a limp.

JOHNNY: Daybreak is a happy time. **[Regards LOUISE.]**
Lonely eyes but sociable fat legs, white and cold like dead
chickens.

CLIVEY: Listen mate, shut up about her legs right!

LOUISE: Well it's given me a limp, and my knees are like jelly.

CLIVEY: Well I don't know what it is do I? You drink too
much.

LOUISE: Where's your new girlfriend then?

CLIVEY: Leave it out Louise.

LOUISE: Did she get bored with you?

CLIVEY: Are you going to help me up? I'm in pain you know.

LOUISE: Yeah.

CLIVEY: Nobody thinks it's important because there's too much else going on. But what if it happened to you eh? You'd be like this lot – useless. You want to get yourself a pair of these [crutches]. At least I get about.

LOUISE: Yeah you get about all right.

CLIVEY: You think I look like a spider don't you, like this geezer does. You're afraid of me on these because I can move. You'd like me to sit on my arse like you. Like her! [Points to ELLIS.] Like all of this lot, hopeless. Look at them all, just tilting towards that pavement. Eternal Sleep, that's what they want. Well not me. I like to be fast, I want a bit of pace. Do you get me Louise, I can't hang around. I wouldn't like to see you in ten years' time. What a state! Can you pass me my crutch now please?

JOHNNY: You've broken the poor young lady's heart with your cruel words. Have you no mercy?

CLIVEY: Mercy? I can't even walk without sticks these days. [Goes out.].

JOHNNY: Ah, foot strikes bleeding corpse. No, surely not. Who's this?

PEDRO: This is Martin's sister.

JOHNNY: Who's Martin?

PEDRO: This is Martin. He collects things in a jar, like Eeyore.

JOHNNY: [Looking down at ELLIS] Has she jumped out of the window again? It must have got too hot for her. Come on, sit her up, get her legs moving.
[PEDRO just stares at him with his head tilted back.]
All right I'll do it myself.
[JOHNNY pulls ELLIS up by her armpits to a sitting position and props her against a wall.]
We'd better be careful though, those people who rode past just now nearly knocking me over, they're keeping watch for this sort of thing. We are not alone. No. They're going to roll our eyes into the gutter. And who's going to stop them eh? [To PEDRO] I don't like your look. Do you want to come and try me eh?

PEDRO: [Spasm, at which JOHNNY flinches.] Weak arms. I've got weak arms. But I could always boot you in the balls. Couldn't I eh? [Spasm.] Martin. [Limps over to MARTIN.] Let me use those. [Takes binoculars. Spasm. Looks up at the sky. To JOHNNY.] Come and look at the Sun and the Stars. [Pause.] Come on.

JOHNNY: All right, I will. [Points to ELLIS.] She's a friend of mine. She wants me to make her happy.

[A blue light goes by silently.]

PEDRO: Forget about her. Look up there.

JOHNNY: [Looks through the binoculars.] Yes, yes.

PEDRO: Now, tell me. How can you live in a place like that and be such a nigger?

JOHNNY: It's not for us.

PEDRO: Who is it for then?

[A blue light goes by silently. JOHNNY, forgetting the question, starts looking about him, sees ELLIS and goes to her again.]

[Trying to keep his attention.] Look, look, Martin and I were trying to find some er ... treasure, we were looking for treasure you know and em, we were looking for a crate. Now it could have been up there, up in the stars; listening? Or it could have been ... well under a pyramid. Or at the bottom of a wishing well. Do you think we found any? Eh? Was that likely? [Shows him the box.] Was it?

JOHNNY: I'm busy.

PEDRO: No, no, not busy. [Spasm.] Come on old cock, spill the beans. What's the opinion? The answer isn't in her fucking hair is it!

JOHNNY: I'm –

PEDRO: There's just blood in her hair, no answers up there. Maybe you should look in her pants, or have you already looked there?

JOHNNY: I'm a lonely old man.

PEDRO: Don't start grovelling.

JOHNNY: Where did you get that?

PEDRO: It's something she dropped.

JOHNNY: It belongs to someone else I think. I think Ellis found it didn't she, amongst some rubbish.

PEDRO: Who knows?

JOHNNY: It's just like her.

PEDRO: Is it?

JOHNNY: She might be in trouble I suppose.

PEDRO: Who isn't? [Spasm.]

[JOHNNY goes to ELLIS and shakes her until she wakes up. A blue light goes past. We hear the ambulance motor idling as it crawls past.]

JOHNNY: Ellis, wake up!

ELLIS: [Exhausted] I can't move Johnny.

JOHNNY: Of course you can.

LOUISE: Come on love, lift up. [Crouches down.]

ELLIS: I can't, I can't I'm finished.

JOHNNY: Where've you been? I've been holding a conversation and you weren't there. This girl despises me, but I had to tell someone.

ELLIS: Sorry Johnny.

JOHNNY: You look ill. You're not ill are you?

ELLIS: No, I don't think so.

JOHNNY: You're not smiling, there's blood under your nose mixed with snot, it doesn't look very nice.

ELLIS: I'll wipe it.

JOHNNY: Your eyes have turned to water and your shirt's undone.

ELLIS: I've been in love Johnny.

JOHNNY: I've decided that this evening, if we make it, if fortune doesn't mind grinning on us just for a second, if we do, then you would be welcome, you would be very welcome to come to my bedsitting room and re-arrange the plates.

ELLIS: It's too late.

JOHNNY: I would lie on my back and you could put your hand on my chest, and we would sleep and dream together.

79

ELLIS: It's too late, I can't come back with you now Johnny.

JOHNNY: It doesn't matter we won't make it anyhow.

ELLIS: Do you know what a volcano is?

JOHNNY: I haven't seen one but I've heard.

ELLIS: They have mud and blood don't they, running down their cheeks.

JOHNNY: Who is it?

ELLIS: He returned from the sea, I thought he was buried in the depths. I wasn't ready. I was low, you know what I mean don't you Johnny?

JOHNNY: I don't know Ellis.

ELLIS: Then in a forgetful moment I told him I'd had a baby. 'Where is it?' he said. 'Where is it?' I said. 'Yes, where is it?' He was so angry. Isn't that peculiar? I promised I'd try to find it.

[MARTIN turned the gaze of his binoculars upon her. She staggers up to him, and peeps underneath them until he lowers them.]

Is that you?

PEDRO: Is that you Martin?

MARTIN: [To PEDRO] Is that you?

PEDRO: This is your sister Martin.

ELLIS: Martin.

[MARTIN smiles at her.]

I saw you yesterday and I followed you. [Looks round to the others.] But he gave me the slip.

PEDRO: That's not very brotherly is it?

ELLIS: This is Turtle my brother. He goes on holiday to the seaside sometimes. Here it is, take it with you, I said, I can't bear it. Please Martin, little brother.

JOHNNY: That's enough. If you lived with me you'd forget it. You'd only have to open your eyes and I'd be right in front of you. We could lie to each other, avoid each other's eyes, anything.

ELLIS: Of course I regretted it. I ran after him all the way down the dark paths, I couldn't find him . . . But I did, by the sounds of the waves, I found him there bathing his feet in the foam in the dark with some box or other under his arm like treasure! 'Where's my baby?' I screamed. 'It's OK,' he said, poor Turtle, he'd left it someway up the beach safely with his own shoes, His Own Shoes!

PEDRO: [Goes up to LOUISE.] These are our last few moments together. Dance with me.

LOUISE: [In greeting] All right.

PEDRO: Don't be like that. Tell me what you're doing here. Surely you could have waddled off after the Human Spider?

[LOUISE shakes her head.]

Then these are our last few moments together. Dance with me.

[LOUISE shakes her head.]

Come on, I'm longing for a little light relief. [Tries to pick her up.]

LOUISE: No, I can't.

PEDRO: Why not?

LOUISE: My legs.

[PEDRO jerks her to her feet and hugs her to him, she hangs around him like a deadweight.]

PEDRO: Right, this is it. Where's the music?

[The ambulance arrives. A very loud engine noise and a siren, a blue light, slamming of doors, the ambulance crew come, played by the same actors as MARY and CLIVEY.]

AMBULANCEMAN: Good evening, any trouble?

PEDRO: No.

AMBULANCEWOMAN: A caller said there were some people here unable to move.

PEDRO: Nonsense, we're all moving.

AMBULANCEWOMAN: What's the matter with her?

PEDRO: Who?

AMBULANCEWOMAN: The girl around your neck.

PEDRO: Oh her, she's very tired. [Lets her drop to the ground.] Look she's fallen asleep.

[AMBULANCEMAN goes towards LOUISE, but PEDRO

steps over her putting himself between LOUISE and the AMBULANCEMAN.]

AMBULANCEMAN: Let's see.

PEDRO: She's doing fine. It's been a trying evening. You can examine me if you want. Here look into my eyes, my ears. Nothing but wax everywhere, I'm like a candle.

AMBULANCEMAN: Just calm down a minute. Let's have a look over here.

PEDRO: No, you can't, everyone's fine.

AMBULANCEWOMAN: Have I seen you before?

PEDRO: No. Listen tell me something, have you taken any children in tonight? They were very ill, they said the ceiling was purple, they said I was an evergreen . . . No?
[AMBULANCEWOMAN shakes her head.]
Maybe another ambulance?

AMBULANCEWOMAN: It's possible.

PEDRO: There seem to be a lot of them. **[Spasm.]**

AMBULANCEMAN: What?

PEDRO: Circling around.

AMBULANCEMAN: That's because we're looking for something.

PEDRO: What? **[Spasm.]**

AMBULANCEMAN: Show him the photograph.

AMBULANCEWOMAN: **[Shows him a photo.]** Seen it?

PEDRO: I . . . what is it?

AMBULANCEMAN: It's a box isn't it?

PEDRO: A box.

AMBULANCEWOMAN: Look there it is! **[Spies the box which PEDRO has put by ELLIS.]**

AMBULANCEMAN: Quick get it!

AMBULANCEWOMAN: Ha! This is it all right!

AMBULANCEMAN: Shake it and see.

AMBULANCEWOMAN: **[Shakes the box.]** Oh yes it couldn't be anything else.

AMBULANCEMAN: **[To PEDRO]** Do you know what's in here?

PEDRO: Treasure. **[Spasm.]** Stolen I admit . . . But treasure

all the same. What good is there in life if you can't strike
it lucky every now and again eh?

AMBULANCEMAN: What if we ask these people over here?

PEDRO: Ask away.

**[PEDRO steps aside but then suddenly tries to strangle
the AMBULANCEMAN who expertly elbows PEDRO's
guts and continues towards ELLIS, LOUISE and
JOHNNY.]**

AMBULANCEMAN: **[To MARTIN]** You've got a scar.
It's a big'un. Who did that to you?

AMBULANCEWOMAN: His mother I bet.

AMBULANCEMAN: Your mother burn you up a bit did she?

AMBULANCEWOMAN: **[To JOHNNY]** Can you help us do
you think?

JOHNNY: Yes, I think so.

AMBULANCEWOMAN: **[Indicates ELLIS.]** Looks like this
young lady here isn't capable of walking anymore.

JOHNNY: Yes, it looks that way certainly.

AMBULANCEWOMAN: **[Leaning to ELLIS.]** Hello love. All
right are you?

[ELLIS stares ahead of her.]

She doesn't look well does she?

JOHNNY: No she doesn't.

AMBULANCEMAN: How about you, how are you feeling?

JOHNNY: I ... I'm OK.

AMBULANCEWOMAN: How about if you come with her to
keep her company?

AMBULANCEMAN: There that would be nice wouldn't it?

AMBULANCEWOMAN: You can hold the box.

AMBULANCEMAN: Know what's in it?

AMBULANCEWOMAN: You people don't know what you're
doing do you?

AMBULANCEMAN: You're a bit of a plague. From the little
ones' points of view I mean.

AMBULANCEWOMAN: The children. Children aren't safe in
your hands are they?

AMBULANCEMAN: It's a blooming crime what you've done
between you.

AMBULANCEWOMAN: Look at the load of you.

AMBULANCEMAN: You're not really fit are you? Ask her, go on. Ya, you're not worth the trouble. Let's get the stretcher, take this lot away.

[They go off to fetch stretchers. TINA comes on at the same time carrying Johnny's clothes to her chest.]

TINA: [Throwing the clothes to the ground.] Here they are.

PEDRO: Martin, this is it, she's the treasure. Ask her her name.

MARTIN: [To TINA] Look out!

PEDRO: My friend Martin here wants to go on a big road, where he can get a good look at the cosmos with his binoculars. [Spasm.] You look like a friendly harmless person. That's what he needs. Take him there go on.

[She walks away from him but he follows her grabbing her arm.]

[Spasm.] You're the caring type aren't you? You care. Don't you? Eh? [Goes and drags MARTIN forward.]

TINA: No.

PEDRO: There you are Martin, she doesn't care. But she will, work on her. Take him to see the stars whatever your name is. Take him.

JOHNNY: You haven't washed these have you?

TINA: I'll do them I promise. Here give them. I forgot. [Takes them.]

JOHNNY: It doesn't matter. Give them back.

TINA: [Clutching them.] No.

[TINA stumbles into ELLIS.]

ELLIS: Was that your baby outside? I thought I recognized him.

TINA: Did you see him?

ELLIS: It's all right though. Help is on its way.

TINA: Is it?

ELLIS: They're bringing a stretcher.

TINA: Oh good.

ELLIS: They'll be here in a minute. I was a mother once. It isn't easy. When I dream about him we do this dance. He starts off really small like a little baby turtle then he grows and gets as big as a dinosaur then he starts crawling across a map of the world until he ends bumping into these little planets with his little snout, out there in the cosmos.

PEDRO: Go on Martin take her hand!

JOHNNY: I'd give anything to be somewhere else. I've been training my legs to run but they won't. All those years. We haven't got long.

[The AMBULANCE CREW returns carrying a stretcher.]

PEDRO: Who's holding my hand? Here comes the battering ram.

£   £   £

FOR THE BEST IN PAPERBACKS, LOOK FOR THE

In every corner of the world, on every subject under the sun, Penguin represents quality and variety – the very best in publishing today.

For complete information about books available from Penguin – including Pelicans, Puffins, Peregrines and Penguin Classics – and how to order them, write to us at the appropriate address below. Please note that for copyright reasons the selection of books varies from country to country.

In the United Kingdom: For a complete list of books available from Penguin in the U.K., please write to *Dept E.P., Penguin Books Ltd, Harmondsworth, Middlesex, UB7 0DA*

In the United States: For a complete list of books available from Penguin in the U.S., please write to *Dept BA, Penguin, 299 Murray Hill Parkway, East Rutherford, New Jersey 07073*

In Canada: For a complete list of books available from Penguin in Canada, please write to *Penguin Books Canada Ltd, 2801 John Street, Markham, Ontario L3R 1B4*

In Australia: For a complete list of books available from Penguin in Australia, please write to the *Marketing Department, Penguin Books Australia Ltd, P.O. Box 257, Ringwood, Victoria 3134*

In New Zealand: For a complete list of books available from Penguin in New Zealand, please write to the *Marketing Department, Penguin Books (NZ) Ltd, Private Bag, Takapuna, Auckland 9*

In India: For a complete list of books available from Penguin, please write to *Penguin Overseas Ltd, 706 Eros Apartments, 56 Nehru Place, New Delhi, 110019*

In Holland: For a complete list of books available from Penguin in Holland, please write to *Penguin Books Nederland B.V., Postbus 195, NL–1380AD Weesp, Netherlands*

In Germany: For a complete list of books available from Penguin, please write to *Penguin Books Ltd, Friedrichstrasse 10 – 12, D–6000 Frankfurt Main 1, Federal Republic of Germany*

In Spain: For a complete list of books available from Penguin in Spain, please write to *Longman Penguin España, Calle San Nicolas 15, E–28013 Madrid, Spain*

Edward Albee **Who's Afraid of Virginia Woolf?**

Alan Ayckbourn **The Norman Conquests**

Bertolt Brecht **Parables for the Theatre (The Good Woman of Setzuan/The Caucasian Chalk Circle)**

Anton Chekhov **Plays (The Cherry Orchard/The Three Sisters/Ivanov/The Seagull/Uncle Vanya)**

Michael Hastings **Tom and Viv**

Henrik Ibsen **Hedda Gabler/Pillars of Society/The Wild Duck**

Eugène Ionesco **Absurd Drama (Rhinoceros/The Chair/The Lesson)**

Ben Jonson **Three Comedies (Volpone/The Alchemist/Bartholomew Fair)**

D. H. Lawrence **Three Plays (The Collier's Friday Night/The Daughter-in-Law/The Widowing of Mrs Holroyd)**

Arthur Miller **Death of a Salesman**

John Mortimer **A Voyage Round My Father/What Shall We Tell Caroline?/The Dock Brief**

J. B. Priestley **Time and the Conways/I Have Been Here Before/An Inspector Calls/The Linden Tree**

Peter Shaffer **Amadeus**

Bernard Shaw **Plays Pleasant (Arms and the Man/Candida/The Man of Destiny/You Never Can Tell)**

Sophocles **Three Theban Plays (Oedipus the King/Antigone/Oedipus at Colonus)**

Arnold Wesker **The Wesker Trilogy (Chicken Soup with Barley/Roots/I'm Talking about Jerusalem)**

Oscar Wilde **Plays (Lady Windermere's Fan/A Woman of No Importance/An Ideal Husband/The Importance of Being Earnest/Salome)**

Thornton Wilder **Our Town/The Skin of Our Teeth/The Matchmaker**

Tennessee Williams **Sweet Bird of Youth/A Streetcar Named Desire/The Glass Menagerie**